Computers and Cultural Diversity

SUNY Series, Computers in Education

Cleborne D. Maddux, Editor

Computers and Cultural Diversity

Restructuring for School Success

Robert A. DeVillar

Christian J. Faltis

State University of New York Press

Published by
State University of New York Press, Albany

© 1991 State University of New York

For information, address State University of New York
Press, State University Plaza, Albany, N.Y., 12246

Production by M.R. Mulholland
Marketing by Theresa A. Swierzowski

Library of Congress Cataloging in Publication Data

DeVillar, Robert A.
    Computers and cultural diversity : restructuring for school
success / Robert A. DeVillar, Christian J. Faltis.
        p.   cm—(SUNY series, computers in education)
    Includes bibliographical references.
    ISBN 0-7914-0524-9 (alk. paper).—ISBN 0-7914-0525-7 (pbk.:
alk. paper)
        1. Computer-assisted instruction—United States. 2. Communication
in education—United States. 3. Socially handicapped—Education—
United States. 4. Academic achievement. I. Faltis, Christian.
1950– . II. Title. III. Series: SUNY series in computers in
education.
LB1028.5.D47 1991   90-9668
371.3'34—dc20   CIP

Contents

Foreword

The latter part of the 20th century has been marked by technological changes that are increasingly affecting every facet of human endeavor. This period has also been marked, in North America at least, by a widespread perception among politicians, educators and the general public that schools are failing to provide students with the basic literate and cultural knowledge required to participate effectively in society. An increasing number of students appear to concur with adult perceptions (though for different reasons) regarding the failure of the educational system and express their sense of alienation and frustration by dropping-out prior to completion of high school. Students from historically subordinated minority groups (e.g. black, Hispanic and native American students) are particularly prone to dropping out.

The advent of computers in classrooms across the continent appeared to hold out promise of improved learning for all students and more equitable outcomes for minorities. However, as Robert DeVillar and Christian Faltis lucidly document in this book, there is little evidence that computers and other technological advances are ushering in an era of learning without tears. Many computers lie unused in classrooms either because teachers are intimidated by them or because the available software is unrelated to their curriculum objectives. When computers are used they are more likely to be used for drill and practice activities or to reward students who have finished assignments early than as tools to challenge students to acquire new knowledge and insights. Low-income minority students and girls experience less access to computers and more drill and practice activities than do middle-class white students. The dominant impression one gets is that with the exception of some isolated projects (reviewed in chapters 5 and 6) the technology has had minimal impact on classroom practices. As the authors point out, the typical American classroom still physically segregates learners from each other and promotes individualistic competitive learning in a context where teachers define their roles as transmitters of knowledge and skills to students who, in turn, are given little option but to define their roles in terms of internalizing what is transmitted. Within this context, the role of the computer is as an adjunct transmitter of knowledge and skills.

It is remarkable that virtually none of the "educational reform" reports commissioned in the United States during the 1980s to respond to the "crisis" in American education critically questioned the socio-pedagogical model that dominates American classrooms. In fact, most reports called for measures to increase the intensity of the transmission-internalization duet played out in classrooms across the nation.

DeVillar and Faltis demonstrate cogently how and why such an approach is fundamentally misguided and present an alternative socio-pedagogical framework that conforms both to the imperatives of our rapidly changing social reality and a considerable amount of research data on the outcomes of what they term "positive social interaction" in the classroom. Of particular value is the change of orientation that they emphasize in relation to the computer. Far from being most effective as a tool for promoting individual learning, the computer is now seen as a tool to enhance communication and discovery-oriented learning opportunities for students working cooperatively in small group learning settings.

Within an integrated cooperative context, teachers can unleash the remarkable power of the computer as both a communicative tool and as a tool that provides efficient and flexible access to information required for particular projects or activities. For example, advances in telecommunications allow classrooms across the globe to carry out cooperative projects either as "sister classes" (e.g. the Orillas network) or as participants in conferences on a variety of topics. Compton's and Grollier's encyclopedias are now available on CD-ROM for use by students within the classrooms and schools. In short, access to information has never been easier.

However, in order to make use of the power of the computer as a communicative and discovery tool, students must have some non-trivial reasons for communicating with others and motivation to search out and interpret particular forms of information. In most contemporary classrooms in North America the curriculum has been sanitized such that students are given few opportunities to pursue projects to which they are intrinsically committed. The implicit image of the individual who is supposed to emerge from twelve years of this form of education is considerably closer to a self-centered compliant consumer than to a critical and creative thinker who knows how to cooperate with others in seeking solutions to common problems.

In this book DeVillar and Faltis present an alternative to the continued failure of American education. The student who would emerge from the type of educational experience they espouse is one in which collaborative critical inquiry and creative problem solving are highlighted. How much more appropriate this goal is in view of the cultural and scientific realities of the 21st century! Across North America and Europe demographic changes are occurring that make the culturally and linguistically heterogenous classroom increasingly the norm. Unless students know how to cooperate with students from very different cultural backgrounds they are likely to be both personally and economically disadvantaged insofar as the workplace, whether at managerial or shopfloor level, is becoming similarly internationalized. Thus, traditional classrooms that stress individualized competitive learning are unlikely to prepare students for the realities of living and working in the 21st century.

Similarly, the information explosion makes transmission approaches to pedagogy obsolete. Knowledge is doubling every five-and-one-half years and close to 7,000 scientific articles are written every day. By the time "knowledge" gets selected for inclusion in a curriculum (by no means a politically neutral process), written up in a form suitable for particular groups of students, internalized by teachers and transmitted to students, much of what is finally internalized by students is likely to be obsolete or irrelevant. What makes much more sense is to choose issues or topics in consultation with students and organize the classroom so that students carry out research designed to generate additional insights or knowledge. The conceptual framework presented by DeVillar and Faltis shows how this process can be organized in the classroom and its impact enhanced by appropriate forms of technology. Their approach has implications far beyond the classroom; in fact, cooperation across cultural and national boundaries together with the creative use of technology may be crucial elements in our continued survival as a human race.

Jim Cummins
Toronto, April 1990

Introduction

Schooling, as the most important formal socialization institution within our modern society, is responsible for preparing students to become educated and productive adults, a national goal supported by democratic principles upon which this country was founded. As schools in this country are extraordinary in their racial, ethnic, language and income heterogeneity, achieving this national goal democratically has long been a complex endeavor. Moreover, attempts to capitalize upon heterogeneously-sensitive instruction have not always been at the forefront of mainstream schooling priorities.

Accordingly, students have found themselves in many instances segregated along racial, ethnic and income group characteristics. Such segregation has taken place at the cross-site school level (e.g., school attendance by racial, ethnic, or income status), as well as at the within-site school level (e.g., instruction determined by tracking and/ or ability-grouping of peers within a particular school site) (National Coalition of Advocates for Students, 1985). Remediation efforts at the societal level to change this practice have been confounded by repeated, yet ambiguous, legislative attempts to rectify social inequities while preserving the rights of the individual. In a similar vein, at the school level, classroom instruction has traditionally adhered to a whole-class, competitively driven methods rather than instructional practices designed to address classroom heterogeneity.

As a result of this complex schooling reality, many individuals, and more significantly, groups have experienced negative educational consequences. One highly visible manifestation of negative schooling experiences is, of course, not completing secondary school. For example, in the adjoining cities of Reno and Sparks, Nevada, 32 percent of all black students, 59 percent of Hispanics, and 69 percent of Native Americans do not graduate from high school (Reno Gazette-Journal, September 13, 1989, p. 1). Nationwide drop-out rates for black students are slightly less than twice as great as for white students; those for Hispanics are more than two times as great (National Coalition of Advocates for Students, 1985, p. xi). Aside from cutting against the grain of democratic principles and from the narrow limitations that incomplete education imposes on individual and groups, the societal toll taken on national production and re-source development is unacceptable.

To summarize, segregated and incomplete education have pre-vented particular groups from fully realizing their educational poten-tial, which in turn makes upward mobility exceedingly difficult. This type of education has also precluded particular groups from full representation and participation in political, social and economic institutions. The difficulties faced by particular individuals and groups also negatively influence their self-perceptions as well as the ways they are perceived by others, resulting in practices that reinforce segregation. The inability of individuals and groups from diverse cultural and social backgrounds to work together cooperatively also negatively impacts our national image and our efforts to sustain a critical pace of national development. Accordingly, alternatives which promote the continuation and completion of formal education for all individuals and groups, and which, in turn, enhance societal produc-tivity, remain a national priority.

The Computer as an Educational Alternative

Over the past decade, the presence of microcomputers in schools has become virtually ubiquitous. Their use has been especially touted as an effective means to provide underachieving students remedial assistance through drill and practice (Office of Technology Assess-ment, 1988). Many educators believe that these programs enable underachieving students to rapidly and effectively learn the basic reading, writing, and mathematics skills required for academic suc-cess. Thus, the computer is heralded as a viable alternative to providing the kind of educational experiences that at-risk students need to complete their schooling. Other uses of computers in the school are enrichment-oriented, capitalizing upon the students' abil-ity to exercise greater control over their learning by composing their own computer programs. One of the most well-known illustrations of this type of computer use at the elementary school level is Logo.

Computer use in its present state of development, however, is not universally accepted as an educational alternative capable of ad-dressing the needs of a wide variety of learners. Empirical evidence has not wholly supported the effectiveness of computers to remediate or enrich educational experiences (Becker, 1987; Maddux, 1989). Moreover, a number of educational researchers have pointed out the inequitable distribution and uses of computers along racial, language, gender, and ability lines (see for example, DeVillar & Faltis, 1987; Maddux & Cummings, 1987; OTA, 1988; Arias 1990).

Plan of the Book

This book offers an alternative conceptual framework for effectively incorporating computer use within the heterogeneous classroom. Our framework integrates Vygotskian social learning theory with Allport's contact theory and the principles of cooperative learning. For each of these three major areas, we have identified a corresponding essential element, which are, in respective order: communication, integration, and cooperation. Our fundamental premise is that in a heterogeneous classroom integration necessarily precedes learning, yet each element unequivocally relies upon a prior communicative commitment to talk and work together cooperatively.

The element of communication stresses the social basis of learning through talk. Thus, in the heterogeneous classroom, it is paramount that students talk with their teachers and among themselves in order to enhance their individual and collective learning experiences. However, for verbal interaction of this type to occur in the heterogenous classroom, students, as well as their teachers, must be socially integrated within the same physical setting. Lastly, talk and social integration in the heterogeneous classroom must be complemented by consciously structured cooperative learning practices.

We contend that the three essential elements of communication, integration, and cooperation provide the conceptual framework for effective computer-integrated instruction, and more broadly, for instruction in general. In Part I of the book, entitled *On Communication, Integration and Cooperation in the Heterogeneous Classroom*, we draw upon historical as well as current research-based literature to present a comprehensive analysis of each of the three elements. Chapter 1 opens with a discussion of the effects of grouping strategies on language use in the classroom, and then presents the theoretical ideas of L.S. Vygotsky concerning the role of social interaction in socioacademic learning. The chapter examines the benefits of peer interaction for social, conceptual, and language learning, with a special section devoted to second language acquisition.

Chapter 2 draws attention to the need for social integration in the heterogeneous classroom before students can be expected talk and work together. The chapter begins with a discussion of historical efforts to segregate students along racial and social lines, and then moves on to examine recent attempts to resegregate students through less obvious, but equally objectionable means. The chapter sets the stage for the kinds of problems that come into play when students from diverse racial and cultural groups are physically and socially integrated to talk and work together cooperatively.

Chapter 3 analyzes cooperative learning primarily in light of Allport's contact theory, which posits minimal criteria for the effective integration of students from diverse racial and social groups. The chapter also discusses other formidable constraints on positive interdependence and the exchange of ideas and information during cooperative groupwork in heterogeneous classrooms.

Part II, *Learning Theory and Computer-Integrated Instruction*, shifts attention to the computer-integrated classroom in order to examine the extent to which the three elements of communication, integration, and cooperation are incorporated in the development of theory and practice for computer uses in the school. In chapter 4, we describe the philosophical bases of modern-day computer-integrated instructional practices. Chapter 5 offers a conceptual analysis and critique of current uses for computers in the schools. The critical question posed for each of the practices we analyzed and critiqued was always the same: In what ways does the practice presented in the literature address communication, integration, and cooperation among students of diverse racial and cultural groups?

The final chapter of the book, chapter 6, analyzes the use of computers for remediation purposes and describes several enrichment-oriented trends in computer-integrated instruction within heterogeneous classrooms. With respect to the latter, we discuss the uses of telecommunications, small-group writing projects, and other innovations especially well-suited for the heterogeneous classroom. We conclude the book with a summary statement which reinforces the need for integration, communication, and cooperation as minimal requirements for effective socioacademic achievement in the computer-integrated, heterogeneous classroom.

Part I

On Communication,
Integration,
and Cooperation
in the Heterogeneous Classroom

Organizing the Classroom
for Communication and Learning

Language is the primary vehicle through which students learn concepts and acquire subject matter knowledge. As language is a social phenomenon, it follows that classroom learning occurs through social interaction involving the teacher and/or more capable peers (Tharp & Gallimore, 1988). In this chapter, we discuss the relationship between classroom talk and student learning, first by examining the effect of grouping strategies on language use, and second by presenting the ideas of L.S. Vygotsky concerning the inherently social nature of learning. In subsequent chapters we analyze and discuss the prerequisites for social interaction: integration and cooperation on the part of all students. Without the strong presence of these two inherently social phenomena, there is little chance for social interaction in the classroom, either between the teacher and the students or among the students themselves; moreover, their absence fuels a system of instruction that favors segregation along ethnic, racial, and socioeconomic lines and invites competition among students for the limited resources of learning. In arguing for the primacy of social interaction in learning, and that integration and cooperation make social interaction possible, we are presenting what we consider to be the *minimal necessary conditions* for learning with the assistance of computers. Other important considerations such as the extent to which the content and use of software for any number of purposes (e.g., programming, text editing, drill and practice, simulation) challenges students' intellectual abilities will be discussed in chapter 4.

An Overview of Social Interaction in the Classroom

The use of social interaction as a means to more effectively engage students in purposeful communication and thereby enhance their learning opportunities is a concept historically articulated within U.S. educational philosophy. Dewey (1916), for example, advocated *contexualized learning,* that is connecting language to the shared experiences of students and avoiding dependence upon the instructional practice of teachers telling students about experiences:

> That education is not an affair of "telling" and being told, but an active and constructive process, is a principle almost as generally violated in practice as conceded in theory...Not that the use of language as an educational resource should lessen; but that its use should be more vital and fruitful by having its normal connection with shared activities...with the instrumentalities of cooperative or joint activities. (p. 38)

Social interaction occurs in most classrooms, however, it rarely resembles the kinds of talk found in other settings where activities are pursued cooperatively or jointly. In settings outside the school, children do not idly compile knowledge in the form of isolated facts presented by a single, non-intimate adult, rather they gain it through a dynamic process which depends on social interaction with adults as well as peers. Alvarez (1991), in an ethnographic study of Mexican origin young children's language development at home and in school, found that parents and older siblings regularly interacted with the younger children, frequently adjusting their speech in order to sustain conversation with them. This study shows that in natural settings, children's learning stems from repeated interactions in which meaning and understanding, rather than being taken for granted, are continually and purposefully negotiated through talk.

Classroom interaction, unlike talk occurring in natural settings, is planned for and controlled by one individual, the teacher. One of the teacher's major responsibilities in organizing instruction is to determine what will be talked about, who gets to talk about it and for how long. Cazden (1988, p. 30) presents a representative example of interaction in a classroom dominated by teacher talk and then contrasts it with a similar sequence that might take place in a communicative encounter:

Classroom Talk		Conversation	
Teacher:	What time is it, Sarah?	Speaker A:	What time is it, Sarah?
Student:	Half past two.	Speaker B.	Half past two
Teacher:	Right	Speaker A:	Thank you.

Although the structure in both instances is the same, the motivation for asking the question in the first place is entirely different: the teacher wants the student to display knowledge in order to evaluate it; Speaker A, on the other hand, actually wishes to know the time, and thus B's response is meaningful as can be seen in the way speaker A acknowledges speaker B for having shared the information with him. Speaker B was not necessarily restricted to a short answer, and could have provided additional information, such as "Half past two, but my watch is always a bit fast." In contrast, any response by the student other than the expected one would have been rejected as an error.

The kind of classroom interaction referred to in the example above occurs most often within a grouping strategy in which the majority of instruction is directed simultaneously to all students and in which students are called upon individually to display their knowledge via short answer responses. This grouping strategy is commonly referred to as whole class instruction.

Whole class instruction. In the whole-class instructional setting, teachers do most of the talking throughout the development of a lesson (Flanders, 1970; Goodlad, 1984). When the teacher is talking to the class as a whole, verbal contributions by students are limited both quantitatively and qualitatively, since the primary purpose of learning is the acquisition of teacher-generated facts. Consequently, talk under these circumstances does not enjoy a "normal connection to shared activities" (Dewey, 1916, p. 38).

When instruction is geared to the whole class, the amount of student talk time within a fifty minute class period, is limited to less than one half of a minute per student (Long & Porter, 1985), if we assume an equal distribution of talk opportunities. However, this amount of talk time is based upon the assumption that all students are native speakers of the language used by the teacher. This assumption is questionable in light of the fact that in 1980 the number of limited English proficient school-aged children was estimated to be near 2.4 million (GAO). Without including the children of undocumented workers, this figure is projected to reach the 3.5 million mark by the year 2000 (Trueba, 1989) making the linguistically diverse classroom the rule rather than the exception. Unfortunately, however, it has been found that in linguistically diverse classrooms, opportunities for talk may be even more limited for certain students, as some teachers tend to interact more often with fluent English speakers than with limited English speakers (Schinke-Llano, 1983). In a recent study conducted in Israel to compare whole group instruction to cooperative learning (the Group Investigation Method), Sharan

and Shachar (1988), for example, reported that whole group instruction was least beneficial for bilingual (Middle Eastern) children in
ethnically diverse classrooms. In their words, this group of children
got "the short end of the stick" in the areas of academic achievement,
social interaction, and verbal-intellectual behavior when they were
taught through whole group instruction (Sharan & Shachar, 1988, p.
101).

One factor contributing to inequitable opportunities for student
talk during whole class instruction is that students are placed in the
position of having to compete with one another for the teacher's
attention. Under this condition, access to interaction with the teacher
depends upon many factors: where the student is seated, past performance, language ability, and eagerness to respond, to name a few.
For example, Faltis (1986) described a high school foreign language
classroom in which the majority of teaching was presented through
whole group instruction. During practice exchanges, the teacher
engaged certain more capable students more often than other students, resulting in disparate opportunities for talk. Faltis referred to
the more capable students as *sway students* because of their ability to
influence the teacher's distribution of talk throughout the development of a lesson. Sway students competed with the less capable
students for access to the teacher in order to gain practice opportunities in the foreign language. The teacher viewed the sway students as
a way to engage in "safe" interaction, talk that would present the
whole class with well-formed examples of the vocabulary and structures under study.

Competition for the opportunity to talk in a whole group setting
also affects the amount of talk that students produce. Student talk
within the whole group setting is expected to be brief, on task, and
consistent with what the teacher has already presented (Mehan,
1979). Accordingly, individual students not only speak less frequently
in whole groups, but they produce a minimal amount of talk when they
do (Dawe, 1934, cited in Sharan and Sharan, 1976). Student talk
during whole group instruction also tends to decline as students
progress through grades. Furst and Amidon (1962), for example, used
the Flanders System of Interaction Analysis (FSIA) to investigate
student talk in low socioeconomic urban, middle socioeconomic urban,
and suburban elementary school systems. Analyzing 160 first-through-
sixth grade classroom observation sessions, the researchers found
that student talk decreased (from 39 percent to 27 percent) as
students progressed through the grade levels and that the percentage
of student talk (high: 39 percent; low: 27 percent) was always lower
than that of the teacher (high: 50 percent; low: 45 percent). Furst and

Amidon pinpointed the third grade year as behaviorally different for both teachers and students and as reflective of the student-teacher interaction pattern in their remaining elementary school years. In the third grade, teacher talk increases, teacher praise of students decreases markedly, as does teacher acceptance of students' ideas. Moreover, teachers spend more time giving directions and ask fewer questions in response to student-initiated talk. Student talk, whether in response to the teacher or student initiated, occurs less often.

The decrease in student talk as students progress through the grades appears to be related to the fact that the amount of time students spend in whole group instruction increases from the lower to the upper grades. However, regardless of the grade, teacher-talk commonly exceeds collective pupil-talk throughout the students' schooling experience. Thus, as students grow increasingly able to expand their vocabularies and to manipulate and articulate complex language and thoughts, the opportunities to engage in meaningful classroom conversations which would develop these skills decrease. Pankratz (1967), for example, studied the verbal interactions of ten physics teachers from ten different high schools with their twelfth grade pupils and found that student-talk accounted for less than twenty percent of the total talk in the classroom. Cuban (1984), using his own and national data (i.e., National Science Foundation's *Case Studies in Science Education,* 1978; Sirotnik, 1981), confirms that teachers continue the pattern of dominating talk in ever-increasing percentages as students progress through school, not only in the sciences, but in math and social studies as well (cf. Cuban, 1984, pp. 217–230).

As we have shown, whole group instructional talk is reserved almost exclusively for the teacher and opportunities for using language as a learning resource within whole groups decrease greatly as students move up in the grades. Students are rarely given the opportunity to give directions, to freely pose questions, to interrupt, or to provide feedback concerning the information conveyed by the teacher (Forman and Cazden, 1985). In other words, classroom talk in whole groups does not allow for the kind of interaction and communicative assumptions present in two-way discourse outside of the classroom.

Goffman (1981) limns the key assumptions underlying communicative events as including the two-way capability of: (1) exchanging interpretable messages, (2) providing feedback within the message exchange, (3) verbally seeking, opening and closing channels of communication, (4) indicating that a message is ended and that another speaker may proceed, and (5) interrupting a speaker in progress. Accordingly, very little of the talk occurring during whole group instruction would meet these communicative assumptions. Since students are rarely allowed to be anything other than passive recipients of teacher-controlled talk, classroom interaction under these circumstances may be more aptly characterized as communicative semblance.

To summarize, within the whole class grouping strategy, social interaction by students remains (1) severely limited and actually diminishes over time in quantity; (2) constrained in quality by an interaction pattern that requires short answers; and (3) unreflective of social interaction patterns present outside the classroom. Although all students are less likely to learn when they are precluded from social interaction, students who are limited in English are at an even greater risk since language acquisition depends greatly on the extent to which opportunities exist for students to use language for communicative purposes (Wong-Fillmore, 1985, p. 26)

Individualized instruction.   Another traditional manner of organizing classrooms for learning is to have students work individually, especially immediately following whole class instruction. This practice has been emphasized over the past twenty years as a means to address differences in styles and rates of learning between individuals. Goodlad (1984) found, however, that although teachers at all grade levels had students work individually, the learning tasks were essentially identical. Thus, accommodation by teachers to different learning styles or rates was not generally evident. Individualized instruction, moreover, led to even less social interaction between teacher and students, and was related to a greater use of worksheets and other prefabricated materials. Clearly, this approach to instruction offers little in the way of communicative practice for limited English-proficient students.

Instruction in many classrooms, therefore, whether organized as a whole class or individualized activity, does not encourage communicative exchanges between students and their teacher. In discussing general trends, Goodlad (1984) reported that students talking in the form of discussion ranged only between four and eight percent of total class time, while listening to teacher's lectures and completing workbook assignments consumed between forty and fifty-five percent of total class time.

Social interaction in bilingual / ESL classrooms.   In bilingual/ English as a Second Language (ESL) classrooms, where special attention is paid to language development, are the patterns of social interaction between students and their teachers different from those found in the majority of regular classrooms? Ramirez and Merino (1990) investigated the nature of teacher and student talk in three types of bilingual education program models: (a) structured English immersion, (b) early-exit transitional bilingual, and (c) late-exit transitional bilingual.[1] They systematically observed one hundred and three first and second grade classrooms at eight sites in California, Florida, New Jersey, New York and Texas. Their findings indicate that across programs and grades:

(1)   teachers organized the classroom for whole class instruction;
(2)   teachers dominated the amount of talk, generating two to three times more talk than students;
(3)   with minor exceptions, teachers did not vary their speech patterns in relation to students' English language proficiency levels;
(4)   teachers used display questions to request simple recall responses from students two-to-three times more often than referential questions, which, if used, would require students to respond with more elaborate language use;
(5)   over 75 percent of student interactions with teachers were in response to teacher initiations;
(6)   student interactions with teachers predominantly were in the form of expected responses (27–36 percent) and nonverbal responses (40–61 percent); free responses accounted for less than 10 percent of all student responding behaviors; and,
(7)   student initiated interactions with teachers accounted for less than 25 percent of all student-teacher exchanges.

In discussing the results, which did not surprise them, Ramirez and Merino (1990) suggest the possibility that both limited language proficiency and cultural rules governing the appropriateness of talk in the classroom could have contributed to the low levels of student-talk. While both possibilities are plausible, the similarity between their findings and the pattern of studentless-talk generally found in regular classrooms, it seems more likely that the social organization of the observed classrooms was mainly responsible for the limited occurrence of social interaction in the service of academic learning.

In summary, the opportunities for students to engage in classroom talk, whether in regular, bilingual or ESL settings, are minimal. The instructional process within the above settings is characterized by teacher-dominated talk, student passivity, rote learning behavior, and rigid adherence to whole and individualized grouping strategies.

In such settings, students participate little in the learning process; their role instead is to receive and recall factual information about which they will subsequently be tested. There are serious problems associated with such an approach to classroom learning, four of the more salient being: (1) the rote acquisition of facts in the guise of knowledge, (2) the general lack of social interaction as an instructional strategy, (3) the promotion of competition as the sole means of gaining access to social interaction with the teacher, and (4) the dependence upon the teacher as sole agent in the transmission and development of knowledge.

Classroom learning under these conditions, in essence, does not reflect the various ways children are assisted to learn in their external environment (see Heath, 1989 for a cross-cultural examination of language learning). In settings outside the school, children do not compile knowledge in the form of isolated facts learned from a single adult model who virtually dominates all talk, rather they gain it through the verbal and contextual assistance of adults as well as peers (Wells, 1985; Alvarez,1991). Greeno (1989) reinforces this point by stressing that learning outside of the classroom is necessarily tied to social events as opposed to merely being an activity in the child's mind.

In the following sections, we present a framework for learning based upon Vygotskian social learning theory. In doing so, we lay out what represents to us the first major condition for effective instruction in computer-integrated classrooms. Specifically, we posit that social interaction through verbal exchanges following Vygotskian principles of communication is required for effective classroom learning. We argue in subsequent chapters that achieving a Vygotskian notion of communication in culturally diverse classrooms depends upon the degree to which language and other minority students are integrated through grouping strategies that encourage all students to talk and work together.

Vygotskian Principles of Communication and Learning

The role of social interaction between children and more mature conversants in individual learning was first explored over sixty years ago by Lev Semenovich Vygotsky (1896–1934), a Soviet educational psychologist. Vygotsky posited that the learning process for children and youth depends upon the presence of four interrelated conditions. The four conditions are as follows:

(1)   the presence of an adult or a more capable peer;
(2)   the occurrence of social interaction between the learner and the adult or more capable peer;
(3)   that interaction be carried out in a language comprehensible to both learners and adults or more capable peers;
(4)   that the adult or more capable peer operate within what Vygotsky called the learner's "zone of proximal development."

For Vygotsky, individual learning can occur only after these social conditions for verbal interaction are met. At the heart of Vygotsky's learning theory is that children's thinking processes reflect the organizational properties of the social life from which they were derived. Thus, a child who has participated in collaborative problem-solving tasks will use the method of solving a problem arrived at collectively when attempting to solve a similar problem individually.

From a Vygotskian perspective, the goal of learning within the classroom is to transform students into independent thinkers through a process which necessarily begins with social interaction mediated by language made comprehensible by an adult or more capable peer. For Vygotsky, learning is a two phase process that first requires a student to receive assistance, mainly through talking with significant others, in order for him or her to complete a particular task. By talking through a problem with someone who fully understands it, the student ultimately internalizes the ability to solve similar problems individually. Resnick (1985) portrays the Vygotskian relationship of social interaction between children and adults to individual learning as one in which "the child does what he or she can, and the adult does the rest." From this perspective:

cognition begins in social situations in which a child shares responsibility for producing a complete performance with an adult. The child does what he or she can, the adult does the rest. In this way, practice on components occurs in the context of the full performance. In naturally occurring interactions of this kind, the adult will gradually increase expectations of how much of the full performance the child can be responsible for (Resnick, 1985, p. 179).

To be effective for learning, adult interaction with children must fall within the zone of proximal development Vygotsky characterized the zone of proximal development as the distance between a child's "actual developmental level as determined by independent problem solving" and the higher level of "potential development as determined through problem solving under adult guidance or in collaboration with more capable peers" (1978, p. 86). Among contemporary students of Vygotsky, the notion of problem solving in this definition has been extended to mean performance on many domains of competence (Cazden, 1981; Tharp & Gallimore, 1988).

Vygotsky argued that the child can operate "only within certain limits that are strictly fixed by the state of the child's development and intellectual possibilities" (Vygotsky, 1934, p. 219 in Wertsch, 1985). Accordingly, the zone of proximal development is a function of both the child's level of development and of the kind of instruction involved. In talking with the child, if the adult structures interaction so that the child can be a successful participant from the beginning, then the adult is working within the child's zone of proximal development. The goal of interaction within the zone is to enable the child, through guided verbal exchanges of ideas, to take on the role of knower (Cazden, 1988).

Within the classroom context, a Vygotskian perspective maintains that social interaction has the greatest learning consequences when the assistance given is presented through talk that is suitably tuned to the student's zone of proximal development (Tharp & Gallimore, 1988). Talk that is tuned to the student's zone of proximal development and done for the purpose of helping the student gain conceptual understanding has two key objectives to satisfy: First, the talk must enable the student to actively participate in interactional exchanges from the outset and second, it must provide support for interaction that is both adjustable and temporary (Cazden, 1988). Because each student has a different zone of proximal development, and because of the difficulty involved in adjusting interaction to a broad range of students at the same time, both teacher-led and peer-driven small groups are the two most promising settings for assisted performance.

Teacher-led social interaction during small group work. One way to effectively provide the support needed for sustained interaction within the zone during teacher-led small group work is through instructional *scaffolds* (Applebee & Langer, 1983; Bruner, 1978, Palinscar, 1986). Scaffolds allow the teacher to assist performance that would otherwise be beyond the learner's individual capacity. Bruner (1978) characterized scaffolds as verbal clues that help learners with conceptual understanding. Within an interactional exchange, a scaffold may appear as a restatement of an appropriate response, as an explicit connection between new and previous information, or as a request for clarification. The need for interactional scaffolds diminishes, as was mentioned above, in direct proportion to the student's growth in understanding and competence.

Assisted performance in teacher-led small group interaction is structurally sustained to the extent that it completes the sequential organization of initiation-reply-evaluation underlying classroom discourse (Mehan, 1979). Of the three elements, evaluating is primarily the responsibility of the teacher; both the students and the teacher can initiate talk and reply to questions. However, as the more capable participant, the teacher is more prone to use initiations and evaluations of replies as scaffolds for learning. Through initiations, the teacher can have students selectively attend to several aspects of the task, and in the process, prepare them for the solution by asking leading questions and explaining unknown terms. When students provide incorrect or incomplete responses, the teacher can sustain the exchange by posing follow-up questions (Au and Kawakami, 1984).

As the teacher interacts with students, one of the most important pedagogical decisions to make is how much assistance to provide in subsequent interactions. The information needed to help make this decision comes primarily from two kinds of teacher questions: (1) assessment questions asked early on during the interaction and (2) assisting questions posed in response to student replies (Tharp & Gallimore, 1988). Assessment questions provide the teacher with information concerning how much social assistance is required in subsequent interaction. Assisting questions, in contrast, actually provide the scaffolds that eventually lead the student to individual learning. Both kinds of questions generate complex as well as simple exchanges (Au and Kawakami, 1984). Complex exchanges require the teacher to support the students' performance through rephrasing, clarifying, and asking follow-up questions. Simple exchanges, on the other hand, require short answers in response to comprehension questions.

Both kinds of questions enable the teacher to utilize what the student appears to understand up to that point as a means to direct the interaction toward *reconceptualization*, which Wertsch (1985) refers to as the acceptance of a qualitatively different understanding of the task at hand. Reconceptualization, therefore, becomes the new goal once an initiation-reply pair has been made. Support for the new goal comes primarily through the process of teacher evaluation which takes the form of *calibration*, the deliberate but temporary adjustment of information provided to the student during the pursuit of new knowledge. Thus, assisted performance involves both a process and product motivation, though in practice this distinction is blurry. As Au and Kawakami (1984) point out, the reason for the fuzziness is because social learning exchanges always involve the use of existing information as a knowledge base. Even though long-term retention of the information may not be the goal of the interaction, teachers make use of the information as they assist students to reconceptualize concepts and propositions embedded in it. The fact that reconceptualization occurs simultaneously serves as an indication that social interaction has successfully guided the students to the acquisition of new knowledge.

To see how social interaction can support individual learning, let us examine two approaches to small group instruction based on Vygotskian principles of teaching and learning. The first approach is called *reciprocal teaching* and is based upon the work of Annemarie Palincsar and Ann Brown (Palincsar & Brown, 1984; Palincsar, 1986; Palincsar, Brown, & Campione, 1989; Brown & Palincsar, 1986). Reciprocal teaching involves the teaching of comprehension-fostering and comprehension-monitoring strategies to poor readers in a small group setting. Palincsar (1986) explains that the instructional format was called reciprocal because:

> "One party acts by way of response or reaction to the second party. Reciprocal teaching is best represented as a dialogue between teachers and students in which participants take turns assuming the role of teacher" (p. 77).

Thus, the teacher and the students take turns leading a dialogue centered on pertinent features of the text. Immediately below, we present an example of the social interaction occurring in a study of reciprocal teaching involving eight first grade teachers, each instructing a small group of six students (Palincsar, 1986). Students in this study received thirty minutes of daily reciprocal teaching for five weeks. They were helped to acquire four different strategies: summarizing, questioning, predicting, and clarifying to help understand the text. We begin with the exchange that took place on Day 4.[2] (Palincsar, 1986, pp. 89–90)

1. T: Today we're going to have a new story about a new animal. We will still be doing the same things. We will try to summarize, we'll ask questions, we'll try to predict, and

we'll also try to clarify any words that you may not understand...The title of today's story is "Cats Do Talk." Any predictions about what you think this story is going to tell us?

2.   S3:   That cats can talk.

3.   T: Exactly, I think that it is going to talk about that. How do you think that they talk, Raul?

4.   S3:   They move their tails.

5.   T: Any other predictions? Let's see if Raul's predictions are right.

6.   S6:   When they want to go out, they scratch on the door. Or, when they want to come in, they scratch on the door.

TEXT: Cats have many ways of "talking." They may not speak words as people do, but cats use sounds and movements to show their feelings. Here are some ways cats communicate.

7.   T: How do cats show their feelings?

8.   S4:   They talk. They make a sound.

9.   T: Did the paragraph tell us about any other way they can talk to you?

10. S1:   They come up to you.

11. T: So, through their movements they can show whether they need something.

12. S2:   They come up to your arm.

13. T: What do you think they are trying to tell you when they come up to your arm?

14. S2:   That they are your friend.

15. T: Very good. If I were to summarize, I would say that this is telling us that cats do talk through using movements and sounds. There is a word here that I'm not quite sure if I quite understand. There was a long word "communicate." [repeats sentence] What does that sentence mean?

16. S1:   Um, talk.

17. T: There are some ways that they talk. All right, so, the talking and the movements let us know something, don't they? So communication is not just talking; it's a way to let us know something. Anna, do you want to try to be the teacher for this next one? I want you to listen and think of a question that you can ask the group.

In this dialogue, the teacher accounts for the majority of the talk. She carefully guides the dialogue by explicitly modeling the strategies she wants the children to learn. She provides extensive support to the students, who at this point are still having difficulty with performing the strategies on their own. For example, when the student's answer falls short, as in line 16, the teacher calibrates by providing an extended definition in the next line, one that incorporates the student's response, but clarifies the meaning inside the student's zone of proximal development. There is one other point to notice. The teacher says "good" only once, in line 15, but, the purpose her is to signal a boundary in the discourse as much as it is to provide positive reinforcement.

Let us now examine the exchange that occurred with the same group of first graders fifteen days later (Palincsar, 1986, pp. 93–95).

TEXT: Behind the front legs, there are two odor glands. They look like two extra eyes. To protect itself, a daddy longlegs can give off a smelly liquid from these glands. Birds, toads, and large insects don't like it at all. It makes them feel too sick or too weak to try to catch the daddy longlegs.

1. S6: [question] What does the daddy longlegs do when something comes around it? Jody?
2. S2: Use that odor and...[not audible]
3. S3: Yeah, Cindy.
4. S2: When an animal comes along, he puts out his odor and they get too sick to catch him.
5. S6: Yeah. Manuel.
6. S4: Or too weak.
7. S3: They feel too weak and too sick.
8. S6: Everybody gave me good answers.
9. T: Very good.
10. S6: [summary] I will summarize. When an animal comes around it, it gives out its bad smell, and they get weak and too old [sic] to catch it...[student-to-student dialogue continues for eleven more lines]

TEXT: Daddy longlegs are related to spiders.

22. S6: What does related mean?
23. T: What do you think, Bobby?
24. S6: Sort of like, they're the same kind of animal, sort of like. Like, tigers are related to cats.
25. T: Very good. They may not be in the same family, but they are similar.

TEXT: Daddy longlegs are related to spiders, but they are not true spiders. Daddy longlegs don't spin webs to trap insects for food the way spiders do. Daddy longlegs go out hunting for

their food. Daddy longlegs never bite people and they are
never poisonous.

26. S1:   [question] Are the spiders ever poisonous or not? Manuel?
27. S4:   They aren't
28. S2:   I did have a different question.
29. T: Okay.
30. S2:   [question and clarification] If the spiders didn't spin a web
for their food, how did they get their food?
31. S5:   Oh, that's a terrific question.
32. T: It sure is, isn't it [dialogue continues for thirty more lines].

Contrasting this dialogue with the one on Day 4, we can see that
the children sustain interaction among themselves fairly independently of the teacher. The examples illustrate how the proportion of
responsibility for task completion shifted from a joint effort, with the
teacher providing the appropriate scaffolds, to an individual effort
where the students came to reconceptualize socially-based knowledge. By Day 19, the students demonstrated a new understanding of
how to perform certain comprehension-fostering and comprehension-
monitoring strategies without the help of the teacher.

The second approach to small group teaching that illustrates
Vygotskian principles of teaching and learning is the *experience-text-
relationship* (ETR) method (Au, 1979; Au & Mason, 1981; Au &
Kawakami, 1984; Au & Kawakami, 1985). In ETR lessons the teacher
models and guide students through the process of using background
knowledge to understand and interpret text. In the experience (E)
phase, the teacher works to bring out the students' personal experiences relevant to the topic of the text to be read. Next, the teacher has
the student silently read a section of the text in order to locate specific
information (e.g., characters and setting). Still in the text (T) phase,
the teacher then discusses the details of the text with the students,
and encourages them to think about what might happen later in the
story. Finally, in the relationship (R) phase, the teacher, using
assessing and assisting questions, helps the students make connec-
tions between their own experiences and the text just read (see Mason
& Au, 1986).

In ETR lessons, reading skills are first practiced by students
under close adult guidance. Accordingly, the teacher is actively
involved in all three phases while students are just beginning to
develop text comprehension abilities. As students gradually become
able to identify and access their own experiences as relevant to the
topic of the story, the teacher can decrease his or her assistance during

the E phase accordingly. As students show an ability to comprehend text, the teacher may also begin to provide less assistance during the T phase. In the final stage, the teacher providing only minimal assistance delegates the majority of responsibility for learning in all phases to the students. We draw from Au and Kawakami's model (1984, p. 212) to depict this gradual transference of skill from the interpsychological to the intrapsychological plane of functioning in the following way:

Stage I: E/T/R (teacher assistance in all 3 phases)

Stage II: (E)/T/R (little or no assistance in E phase)

Stage III: (E)/(T)/R (students able to comprehend text with little or no teacher assistance)

Stage IV: (E)/(T)/(R) (student able to perform all phases with little or no teacher assistance)

Au and Kawakami (1984) examined the interactional processes occurring in one ETR lesson involving a group of five Hawaiian children in Kamehameha Early Education Program in Honolulu, Hawaii (Calfee, Cazden, Duran, Griffin, Martus, & Willis, 1981). The aim of the study was to show the ways in which the teacher's role in guiding instructional interaction assisted students in the development of academic skills. Five research questions were addressed. The first question concerned the number of teacher questions that students had difficulty answering correctly. The researchers expected that there would be a substantial number of interactional exchanges opening with teacher questions that could not be easily answered. If this occurred, it was assumed that teachers were instructing within the zone of proximal development. The results showed that students had difficulty responding to eleven of thirty-four opening questions, leading the researchers to conclude that the teacher was indeed working within their collective zones. The fact that some of the questions elicited correct responses was also important because it enabled the teacher to sustain interaction, as well as prevented the students from becoming overly frustrated.

The second research question examined the teacher's willingness to elicit information from the students rather than merely telling them what they needed to know, even if students had to struggle to arrive at an acceptable answer. The researchers analyzed what the teacher did following incorrect student responses. The teacher could wait for another student to supply a response, ask a question to provide a clue, or reveal the answer. Of the twenty-five incorrect student responses, the teacher waited or ignored the response after eleven, after thirteen she asked an assisting question, and after only one did she reveal the answer. This result lends credence to the Vygotskian principle that children internalize the social conditions of learning. In this case, the students felt comfortable attempting to answer questions even when they were unsure of the correct response, which was precisely the kind of social learning environment the teacher was striving to create.

The third research question concerned the willingness of the teacher to engage in long-term interactions with the students, and have them work for answers. This question was addressed by counting the number of complex versus simple exchanges. It was assumed that if the teacher was eliciting responses from the students, and having them work for answers, then the exchanges around many of the questions should involve one or more follow-up question and several sets of student responses. The results indicated that there were twenty-three complex interchanges and fifteen simple ones. Complex interchanges allowed the teacher to assist the students' comprehension performance. Simple exchanges, on the other hand, were valuable because they allowed the teacher to check comprehension and to establish simple propositions essential for understanding the information in the text.

The fourth research question centered on the teacher's behaviors in reinforcing appropriate student responses, in consistently modelling comprehension processes, and in focusing the discussion. The researchers examined the teacher's behavior at the end of each exchange, looking for two possibilities: did the teacher restate main points or merely acknowledge students' responses? (There was only one interchange in which the teacher did neither.) Results showed that thirty of the exchanges concluded with a teacher restatement, while eight ended with an acknowledgement. Thus, the teacher explicitly marked key information for the students, modeling the kinds of mental notetaking that mature readers do routinely.

The fifth research question had to do with the extent to which students introduced topics for discussion that were not directly cued by a teacher question. The researchers examined each discussion to determine whether it was initiated by a student. They encountered four student initiated interchanges, all of which served as the basis for further group discussion. Accordingly, student initiated talk and its use by the teacher in the ensuing exchanges are both in keeping with

Vygotskian principles of teaching and learning. Similar to reciprocal teaching, as described above, students assumed the teacher's role of initiating talk and generating the next topic for discussion.

The two approaches to small group instruction illustrate the value of assisted interaction, and both point to the necessity of complex as well as simple interchanges for learning to take place as a result of group discussion. Both approaches also indicate the kinds of interactional decisions teachers must make in order to shift the responsibility for learning to the students. In the next section, we examine social interaction among peers talking and working together under the guidance, but not under the direct verbal influence, of the teacher.

Social interaction among peers in small groupwork. There is ample evidence to suggest that interaction among peers of generally equal understanding, but with differing skill preparation, is also a valuable source of learning. Vygotsky intimates the importance of peer talk in small groups in his definition of the zone of proximal development (see page 12), referring specifically to the role "more capable peers" may have in new conceptual understanding. In this context, a more capable peer is a student who, similar to the teacher, possesses certain skill preparation that is particularly appropriate to assisting a fellow student in the completion of a task that is within that student's zone of proximal development.

Cazden (1988) presents four potential cognitive benefits of small group peer interaction, all of which support the Vygotskian notion that the means used for social interaction are taken over by the learner and internalized. The four benefits of interaction are as follows: (1) as a means for a catalyst, (2) as the enactment of complementary roles, (3) as orientation to an audience, and (4) as exploratory talk.

The catalytic function of peer group interaction speaks to the well-documented finding that when children talk and work together, they often present different points of view about the nature of things (see Forman & Cazden, 1985). Followers of Piagetian psychology recognize the value of catalytic talk because of the cognitive conflict that it may stimulate (Perret-Clermont, 1980). For Vygotsky, the value of having students confront an alternative point of view comes from the means by which the conflict is discussed and eventually resolved. Confronting an alternative view allows children to gain control and internalize the means of social interaction, to pose and respond to questions in a fashion similar to how the teacher has interacted with them. Cazden (1988) is quick to point out, however, that among peers, it is not uncommon for conversion to a new point of view to occur gradually, similar to the way children learn their first or second language, rather than immediately as might be expected. For example, Spanish-speaking children learning English as a second language typically pass through several stages of development in the acquisition of English negation (Hernandez-Chavez, 1972). These children will produce utterances such as "I no know it" and "I no like this one" in spite of evidence to the contrary, and after repeated error correction. With rare exception, however, all children eventually acquire the appropriate, adult-like form. Thus, as Cazden (1988) argues, "we have to assume that exposure to alternatives plays a part, even though we can't track their influence in the silent processes of the child's mind" (p. 128).

Peer group interaction in small groups may also lead to the development of complementary roles that are essential to the solution of problems. When students are placed in groups to work together, there is a need to make sure that each member is effectively contributing to the solution of the problem. At the very least, each student has to know what is required of the task. As students explain what to do and how to do it, they take on certain roles which enable them to solve problems together which individual members would be incapable of solving alone.

A third and less widely discussed by-product of social interaction is the multiple audience orientation it can provide. Orientation to an audience is the result of feedback that is given when something said or written is unclear. In whole group instruction, students are limited to virtually one audience, that of the teacher as an examiner who corrects and evaluates what students say (Goodlad, 1984; Ramirez & Merino, 1990). Once students are placed in small groups and allowed to talk and work together, the audience immediately changes to a peer orientation. Each member of the group is free to ask and answer questions about the meaning of what other group members have written or said. When a computer is involved in the task, the computer itself (its software, that is) provides an additional resource for audience orientation, since now the students need to direct their discussion not only in terms of one another, but also to what the computer is outputting. Bruce, Michaels and Watson-Gegeo (1985), for example, report how a sixth grade class in a lower-class urban school in the northeast United States acquired a keen sense of audience as pairs of students worked together on computers to write critical reviews of a show that included a series of songs, one nonmusical skit, and several performances by a mixed grade glee club. Bruce *et al* (1985) found that the students paid attention to each other's writing, often commenting on it as they waited in line to use the computer. Moreover, students talked to one another about the task at hand as they wrote together at the computer. They found that as students began to understand the need to pay attention to the concerns of the audience, their writing improved accordingly. Analyzed in Vygotskian terms, it appears that students internalized the notion of audience orientation through social interaction with others who shared the need to communicate clearly.

Lastly, talk among peers in small groups can promote what Barnes (1976) characterizes as "Exploratory talk." This kind of talk relates to learning in the way it enables students to rehearse their understanding of a topic with a familiar audience, and to do so without paying exclusive attention to external criteria. In exploratory talk, the learner "takes responsibility for the adequacy of his thinking" (Barnes, p. 113). Then, as the lesson shifts back to whole class instruction, where the teacher expects talk to be more refined, students enjoy the advantage of having already explored relevant topics on their own terms.

There are numerous empirical studies which support the value of peer interaction for individual cognitive development. Forman and Cazden (1985) report on a study conducted by Forman which found that in tasks where experimental evidence was being generated through talk and where managerial skills were required, students could perform tasks together before they could perform them alone. Weisner, Gallimore, and Jordan (1988) report that one of the most favorable learning conditions in classrooms containing high numbers of native Hawaiian children is the presence of student-generated interactions that rely on peer assistance for task completion. Garcia's (1990) study of interaction in effective Hispanic classrooms also points to the value of talk among peers. He found that in high-achieving classrooms there was a significant amount of student-dominated interaction. Reporting on the same effective Hispanic classroom project, Moll (1988) commented that in every classroom "teachers emphasized the students' active use of language to obtain or express meaning" (p. 467). Underlying the general purpose of teaching in all the classrooms he observed was an effort to create classroom contexts in which the students learned to use, try out, and manipulate language for real purposes.

Peer Interaction and Second Language Acquisition

While peer interaction in small groups can lead to a number of cognitive and academic benefits, there is another strong justification for including it as a teaching strategy. Peer interaction in small groups generates several of the most important ingredients needed to promote second language acquisition. As was mentioned above, it is estimated that there will be more than 3.5 million limited-English proficient school-aged children by the year 2000. For these children, interaction with fellow students, especially fluent English-speaking peers has the potential to lead not only to cognitive growth, but to language acquisition as well.

Before discussing how peer interaction contributes to second language acquisition, let us briefly examine what needs to be present for learners to become increasingly proficient in a second language. After reviewing some thirty-five studies, Long (1981) concluded that because modified input and modified verbal interaction were present in all cases of successful second language acquisition, they must be among the necessary and sufficient conditions for acquisition to occur. Long's definition of modified input is comparable to Krashen's (1982; 1985) more widely used notion of *comprehensible input*, language addressed to the learner that has in some way been adjusted to accommodate that learner's needs. Adjustment can be in the form of simplified speech that has been slowed down and more clearly enunciated or it can be speech that has been highly contextualized through the use of visual support and/or physical gestures (See Allen, 1986, and Enright and McCloskey, 1988 especially chapters 5 and 6). For Krashen, acquisition takes place when learners understand language that is a bit beyond their current level of competence. Providing learners with language slightly more advanced than their levels of development implies that talk is roughly tuned rather than finely tuned, and as such provides a built-in review as well as brings attention to more advanced aspects of language.

Comprehensible input as Krashen characterizes it shares both a point of commonality and a point of difference with the zone of proximal development. The two constructs are similar in that advancement is possible to the extent that language input is made comprehensible to the learner by an adult or more capable (i.e., more proficient) peer. Moreover, both constructs underscore the importance of being responsive to the learner's perceived needs. The difference between comprehensible input and the zone of proximal development lies in the focus each construct places on the role of language in learning. Whereas comprehensible input stresses the importance of adjusting speech to the learner's linguistic level of competence, the zone of proximal development focuses on adjusting speech to the learner's interactional level of competence.

There is some evidence that language input that is too far beyond learners' current level of ability has no effect on their language development, even though they are able to interact with the teacher. Pienemann (1984), for example, studied ten Italian children who were at stage two or stage three in German as a second language. The ten children, ages seven through nine, were given two weeks of classroom instruction in which structures found in stage four were emphasized in linguistic as well as communicatively oriented activities. The results indicated that children who had started at stage three had progressed to stage four, a process normally requiring several months of unaided, intensive exposure to the second language. Those children who had begun at stage two however, remained at that stage. Pienemann interpreted these findings as evidence that students can only profit from instruction that is within their psycholinguistic range of readiness. Thus, while teaching students something that they are ready to learn can accelerate the rate of progress to the next stage, teaching them something that is outside their range of comprehension cannot make them skip a stage in the acquisition sequence.

Peer interaction and second language acquisition. While comprehensible input is clearly important because it promotes acquisition, it is equally clear that native-like mastery of a second language is possible only when students have opportunities to use the second language for communicative purposes, and to do so under conditions which do not create high levels of anxiety. Hawkins (1988), for example, provided evidence that language-minority children who participated in scaffolded small group interaction with native English speakers showed significant improvement toward native-like proficiency even though the amount of intentional comprehensible input they received was limited to the relatively short span of one instructional period per day. On the other hand, Swain (1985) found that language-majority students enrolled in Canadian second language immersion programs enjoyed maximal second language input that was largely comprehensible, yet none reached what might be considered near-native proficiency levels. She suggested that the reason was directly related to the fact that the students had no opportunities for verbal interaction with native speaker peers, opportunities that would have enabled them to engage in complex and simple interchanges where there is a compelling need to negotiate for meaning in order to communicate effectively. Thus, despite several years of immersion schooling which exposed students to considerable amounts of comprehensible input, because the second language was not used to communicate information, express feelings, argue opinions, and explore ideas, they never developed native-like proficiency. In Wong-Fillmore's words (1985), "In order to learn a new language, learners have to be in a position to engage in interactions with speakers in a variety of social situations, since this is what allows them to figure out what is being said, how the language is structured, and how it is used socially and communicatively by its speakers" (p. 26).

One of the chief advantages of peer interaction in linguistically diverse classrooms is that it potentially offers language learners the chance to hear greater amounts of modified language input than they would if their only source was the teacher in a whole class context. Moreover, McGroarty (1989) suggests that input generated from peer interaction can provide a natural context for greater redundancy in communication as students exchange information. Redundancy improves levels of comprehension because speakers naturally tend to repeat words and rephrase ideas as they attempt to convey meanings.

A second benefit for second language learners potentially stemming from peer interaction is that it provides greater practice opportunities (Enright and McCloskey, 1988). We have already presented evidence that in whole class settings, teachers do most if not all of the talking, meaning that while students may be receiving some exposure to comprehensible input, they are nonetheless passive participants in learning. When students are in pairs or in small groups, there are substantially more opportunities for using language to express meanings, provided that groups are structured in such a way that ensures optimal participation by all group members (see chapter 3 for an extensive discussion of organizing groupwork for equitable participation). In a meta-analysis of research on the effects of peer involvement on second language development, Gaies (1985) found that practice opportunities increased greatly in classrooms using peer grouping strategies. Moreover, he attributed the development of fluency in oral skills to the greater amount of practice that peer interaction offers.

Thirdly, peer interaction can promote what we refer to as *intra-group calibration*. Talking and working among peers can be successful only if the language used in completing the task makes sense. In a small group setting, students are more apt to purposefully adjust their own language or the language of their peers in order to continue with the activity. Calibration is done to achieve greater understanding; when it occurs among peers, moreover, it is less likely to raise the overall anxiety level resulting from students having to talk and work in a second language before they are fully proficient.

While the above benefits may occur as a result of peer social interaction, a number of researchers have pointed out that second language development does not necessarily happen simply because students are placed into small groups. Within a bilingual setting, for example, both Milk (1980) and Neves (1984) found that small groupwork might actually constrain second language acquisition. Milk (1980) noted a *laissez-faire* grouping strategy in which teachers as well as students formed groups which tended to result in matched as opposed to mixed language proficiency levels. That is, Spanish-proficient students were either placed or joined with other Spanish-proficient students. Likewise, fluent English speakers were either placed or joined other fluent English speakers. While matched language proficiency groups enable students to interact verbally and thus to develop conceptually, they do not support second language development since there was little need to make language comprehensible to or sustain interaction with second language speakers.

Neves (1984) also found that verbal interaction between peers, in English and Spanish, appeared to be language proficiency-based rather than task-based. As in the Milk (1980) study, Neves found that Spanish-proficient students spoke Spanish among themselves, while English-proficient students used only English. Those peers designated as having minimal proficiency in Spanish and English essentially were not spoken to in either language by the more proficient speakers and produced less speech than any other language proficiency group.

In both cases, the teachers assumed that second language acquisition and mixed-ability peer interaction in a bilingual classroom setting would occur naturally. This assumption ignores the powerful social forces at work in classrooms characterized by language and cultural heterogeneity. We discuss the nature and extent of social forces on student interaction in the following two chapters. Suffice to say at this point that for talk to occur between and among speakers of different second language proficiency levels, small groupwork must be complemented by other supporting strategies: More specifically talk requires cooperative learning strategies consisting of the following minimal components: (1) training in interpersonal and small group skills, (2) individual accountability for mastering the assigned material, (3) face-to-face interaction, and (4) positive interdependence (Johnson, Johnson, & Holubec, 1986). In chapter 3, we present cooperative learning as a formal methodology for socially integrating students form diverse language and cultural backgrounds.

Summary

This chapter began by describing the traditional pattern of social interaction in the majority of K-12 public school classrooms across the United States. Teachers who work within the traditional pattern dominate classroom talk, deciding when it will occur and who will be allowed access to it. Whether in regular or bilingual/ESL classrooms, this traditional option invariably occurs in whole group and individualized instructional contexts, both of which severely restrict the quantity and quality of two-way interaction between the teacher and student and among the students themselves. Without the opportunity to exchange ideas with adults or more capable peers, students will rarely be challenged to solve problems on their own, since the teacher assumes sole responsibility for the transmission and development of knowledge. From a Vygotskian perspective, teaching necessarily consists of socially-mediated performance within the student's zone of proximal development. Thus, an important concern is how the teacher by assisting interaction can facilitate the student's taking over of the learning activities.

Vygotsky's social learning perspective provides us with a theoretical framework for one of the major conditions for effective instructional we believe must be present in computer-integrated classrooms. With its emphasis on assisting performance and social interaction in the zone of proximal development, the Vygotskian perspective asserts that students working at the computer need to exchange ideas both among themselves and with the computers in order "to gain control of their own abilities as literate thinkers and doers" (Langer, 1987, p. 7). While the exchange of ideas among peers and with the teacher supports conceptual learning in general, we also argue that it can be doubly beneficial to students in the process of learning English as a second language because it can provide them with opportunities to use and hear meaningful language.

The extent to which teachers organize instruction with computers to incorporate a social learning perspective depends greatly on how well they are able to counter the social forces that militate against culturally and linguistically diverse students talking together and assisting one another to solve problems cooperatively. In this chapter, we have explicitly identified social interaction in the classroom as a primary condition for effective learning. We have pointed out its value in language and conceptual development for first as well as second language learners. In the next two chapters, we analyze and discuss the roles of integration and cooperation among students in promoting social interaction in the classroom. Our main arguments are that social interaction in heterogeneous computer-integrated classrooms is most likely to occur when students of diverse cultural and language backgrounds are socially integrated in all aspects of classroom activity, and that social integration is most effectively achieved through cooperative learning. Accordingly, in arguing that social interaction is at the heart of classroom learning, that integration is required for social interaction to occur, and that cooperative learning is a formal means to social integration in the classroom, we are presenting what we consider to be the three *minimal necessary conditions* for effective learning in computer-integrated classrooms. It is to the conditions of social integration and the principles of cooperation that we now turn.

Notes

1. *Structured English immersion programs* refer to content-area instruction given in the second language of the student by teachers who are bilingual in the first language of the student and who also have been trained in second language education. In these programs, the English which teachers use during instruction is expected to be adjusted to the respective English language proficiency levels of the students. In *early-exit transitional bilingual programs*, virtually all language of instruction is English. Formal instruction in the students' first language is limited to one hour per day. Throughout the remainder of the instructional day, the students' first language may be used for clarification and support. Thus, English language development is stressed while the development of the first language is restricted. In contrast, within *late-exit transitional bilingual programs* both the first and second language are distributed equally throughout the instructional process. These programs develop the students' two languages and continue through fifth or sixth grade irrespective of the student's ability to receive instruction solely in English.

2. To enhance readability, we have numbered teacher and student exchanges and have provided student pseudonyms in place of the student initials presented in the original text.

Social Integration within the Heterogeneous Classroom

The previous chapter introduced and discussed the notion of enhancing language and content learning opportunities through adult-child, teacher-student and peer groupings guided by the principles within the social interaction learning model of L.S. Vygotsky. Positing the notion of integrating language and subject matter learning opportunities through teacher-student instruction with that of peer group educational activities has a two-fold purpose: This notion serves to conceptually differentiate the social interaction model from the traditional models of instruction currently practiced and, through the interaction of its elements, identifies a potentially effective educational alternative for all students, especially those at risk of not completing their schooling or of performing below norm throughout their schooling.

Earlier, we addressed a paradox with respect to the aims and practices of education that appears general to the U.S. classroom experience independent of program type: While language, especially in the form of talk, is considered essential to attain and demonstrate subject-matter mastery, talk in the classroom is virtually a teacher phenomenon. When talk is directed at students, it is generally characterized by questions to which short-answer responses are expected (Mehan, 1979). Reliance upon teacher-dominated verbal strategies disengages students from active involvement in their own learning process and constrains the degree of language and subject-matter mastery that they attain, irrespective of ability level or language proficiency designation. The National Assessment of Educational Progress (NAEP), for example, reported in 1985 that students across all grade levels generally lacked the ability to examine, elaborate upon, or explain their ideas relative to a passage read, a deficiency which extended across all socioeconomic levels (NAEP,

1985). For students expected to learn English as a second language within this instructional context, opportunities to hear and practice English are reduced both in time (approximately twenty seconds per student per class period, if student language distribution opportunities were allocated equally) and quality (e.g., syntactically reduced constructions in the form of short-answer responses to known information requests by teacher).

The effects of time and quality problems on academic achievement, however, are compounded for those students whose socioeconomic status is below middle class. In the 1981 NAEP study, for example, literacy performance between urban-advantaged and urban-disadvantaged nine-year-old students was comparable.[1] At the thirteen-year-old level, however, the latter group performed 1–10 percent below their urban advantaged counterparts, and, at the seventeen-year-old level, performed 3–13 percent below their advantaged peers. A similar pattern occurred when comparing the mathematics test scores of a national sample of students. The difference in achievement test scores between advantaged whites and their black and Hispanic disadvantaged counterparts was greater at age seventeen than at age nine (Levin, 1985).

Academic performance disparities between advantaged and disadvantaged student groups within the United States are expected to increase. Presently, estimates indicate that at least 30 percent of U.S. elementary and secondary school students are disadvantaged and that their proportion will increase rapidly, thereby exacerbating the academic performance gap between the advantaged and the disadvantaged unless effective educational alternatives are implemented (Levin, 1985).

In summary, while there can be no doubt that at-risk students are in dire need of effective educational alternatives, such alternatives are also necessary to serve the general student populace. Cooperative learning is an educational alternative theoretically and structurally capable of embodying the social interaction principles presented in chapter 1 and which can benefit all students. However, cooperative learning did not evolve within a vacuum; it has its educational antecedents. It is to this alternative, and its antecedents, that we now turn our attention.

Educational Antecedents to Cooperative Learning

Prosocial behavior: the notion and the need. Groups belonging to different races or ethnic groups within the United States have traditionally experienced problems in successfully communicating and functioning together across racial and ethnic boundaries. At the school level, throughout our history, black and ethnic minority students such as Hispanics have had little opportunity to share the same school or classroom facilities with their Anglo-Saxon counterparts. The practice of maintaining separate institutions according to racial distinctions is historically and legally rooted in U.S. society. The advocacy of institutionalized segregation stems form the last decade of the eighteenth century and prevailed legally to the middle of the present century.[2] The practice of segregation, having been politically embraced to varying degrees by black leaders such as Booker T. Washington and W.E.B. DuBois, as well as by white leaders in the United States, attested to the perceived viability of a segregated democratic society and to the virtual inviability of one based upon integration (cf. J.H. Franklin, 1965; E.S. Redkey, 1969; St Clair Drake, 1965). In states where racial minorities other than blacks resided, schooling opportunities were available only within segregated settings. California, for example, the state with the highest proportion of ethnic minorities, segregated Chinese, Japanese, Indians and Mexicans (this latter group was alternately classified as Indian or white), as well as blacks, from white students for purposes of schooling (Wollenberg, 1978).

From 1896 to 1954, the separate but equal doctrine, sanctioned by the U.S. Supreme Court's decision in *Plessey v. Ferguson* (1896), was especially deleterious to interracial relations (cf. Lockard and Murphy, 1980, p. 65). The support for this doctrine was, moreover, widespread across the educational community. Educators generally accepted the practice of separate but equal education, and seventeen states, together with the District of Columbia, actually established dual systems of public education, while four states reserved the option to do so (G.M. Johnson, 1969; see also C.M. Wollenberg, 1978). Black intellectuals also supported educationally different systems. Booker T. Washington, for example, stressed the need for blacks to receive industrial rather than academic education (E.S. Redkey, 1969). W.E.B. DuBois, in contrast, posited that the floodgates of integration would only open as the result of the cultured and formally educated "talented tenth" of the black population having won the respect of their white counterparts (E. S. Redkey, 1969). Black and white scholars and leaders, then, professed that integration was itself a long term process which would ultimately evolve from (1) accommodation to separate but equal practices combined with different educational tracks based on race, and (2) the elite minorities of both races forming a bond of mutual respect that would serve as a model that the majority of common people, regardless of race, could then emulate. Alain Locke's

(1925) own eloquent conclusion illustrates vividly who the players should be in the move toward integration via social contact and cooperation:

> The fiction is that the life of the races is separate, and increasingly so. The fact is that they have touched too closely at the unfavorable and too lightly at the favorable levels...There is a growing realization that in social effort the co-operative basis must supplant long-distance philanthropy, and that the only safeguard for mass relations in the future must be provided in the carefully maintained contacts of the enlightened minorities of both race groups. (Locke, in Bracey et al., p. 340)

Race, however, was not the only factor responsible for communication difficulties at the societal level. Communication problems extended to the U.S. society in general as a result of the diversity characterizing its population. Allport (1954), in his classic work *The Nature of Prejudice*, for example, reported barriers to communication as the logical extension of diversity:

> In the United States—probably the most heterogeneous and complex society on earth—conditions are ripe for abundant group conflict and prejudice. Differences are numerous and visible. The resulting clash of customs, tastes, ideologies cannot help but engender friction. (pp. 216)

During the decade following the Second World War, however, sufficient research data involving interracial/interethnic subjects, both adult (e.g., R.D. DuBois, 1950; Stouffer et al., 1949) and school-age children (e.g., Clark and Clark, 1947, cited in Aronson and Osherow, 1980), had been accumulated to lead social scientists to generally refute the innocuousness of the separate but equal doctrine and the inviability of integration (cf. Deutscher and Chein, 1948). Allport (1954), moreover, concluded that only cooperation linked to the accomplishment of a common goal could lead to the type of effective communication and understanding necessary to bridge the differences brought about by diversity:

> contact must reach below the surface in order to be effective in altering prejudice. Only the type of contact that leads people to do things together is likely to result in changed attitudes...It is the cooperative striving for the goal that engenders solidarity...[I]n

factories, neighborhoods, housing units, schools, common participation and common interests are more effective than the bare fact of equal-status contact. (p. 264)

Allport's conclusion exhibited an important democratic refinement not readily evident in earlier U.S. social thought. Integration was, in his view, a result of specific interrelated elements in widespread societal co-occurrence: people of all races and ethnic backgrounds, at all levels of society, interacting with each other in group-related activities tied to a common goal in which each member worked toward its achievement.

By the early 1950s, then, the weight of scholarly evidence in the area of the social sciences (in conjunction with political activism in the area of civil rights) presented a formidable challenge to the notion that equality of opportunity was viable through separate but equal institutions. Its influence was felt, moreover, outside the academic community, extending into legal arenas where decisions rendered in favor of integration could hold institutions and individuals accountable for implementing desired, if nontraditional, social practices. The single most important example of this influence was reflected in the decision rendered by the U.S. Supreme Court with respect to *Brown v. Board of Education* (1954), where seven sociological studies were cited in footnote form in support of the court's ruling that, inasmuch as feelings of inferiority were generated through the actually separate but rarely equal doctrine (cf. Klineberg, 1986; Plank and Turner, 1987, p. 589), black children were being denied equal educational opportunity.

Thus, the notion of self-esteem was formally introduced as a factor which influences educational outcomes. And, Allport's admonitions notwithstanding, integration—in this case defined as racially diverse student groups within the same physical educational setting—by itself was considered the means by which self-esteem could be enhanced and parity achieved with respect to the educational outcomes of mainly black students vis-a-vis their white counterparts. Nearly a quarter of a century later, researchers continue to address this one-dimensional concept of physical integration as a means to social integration (cf. Hallinan and Teixeira, 1987). It is not surprising, then, that problems of communication continue to exist between those differing along racial, ethnic minority, language, and socioeconomic status lines.

Segregation and ethnic minorities. Racial designations have been, and continue to be, an important element within the United

States. However, as other groups designated as "white" have also experienced *de jure* or *de facto* segregation or other types of unequal opportunity (e.g., employment, income, etc.), ethnicity (together with gender) have also become labels to identify members of historically excluded groups. Children from these groups have generally experienced extreme difficulty in progressing successfully through school. In fact, the majority of students representing racial and ethnic minority groups in the United States tend to underachieve or fail in school, and abnormally high percentages of them leave school prior to completing high school.

The families from which these children come, whether newly arrived or native born, share a composite profile: they are poor, generally ethnically different from the Anglo-Saxon, undereducated, have a less than proficient command of standard English and sometimes their native language, and tend to live in segregated, urban areas (Davis, Haub, and Willette, 1983; Levin, 1985). Data presented by educational researchers (e.g., Calfee, Avelar La Salle, and Cancino, 1988; Catterall and Cota-Robles, 1988; Cohen and Arias, 1988; Levin, 1985; Moore and Pachon, 1985; Slavin and Madden, 1988) continue to confirm that the academic, income and social gaps between white middle class students and poor and minority students continue to widen despite decades of special educational programs. As school sites tend to be a function of residential patterns, children from these groups are at once concentrated amongst themselves for formal schooling and marginalized from interacting in a learning environment with their more affluent, mainstream, standard-English-speaking counterparts.

Educational consequences of segregation, whether by school or by ability grouping, are severe, enduring and massive, especially in terms of dropout rates and retention policies. Dropout rates for children of poor families, for example, are twice that of the national average, and surpass 50 percent at the economically poorest levels (Catterall and Cota-Robles, 1988; Navarro, 1986). At the adult level, significant percentages of whites (24 percent), blacks (38 percent), Hispanics (52 percent) never complete high school (Catterall and Cota-Robles, 1988). Retention practices in many urban schools systematically retain 20 to 25 percent of children in each of the elementary grades (Slavin and Madden, 1988), while other schools have held back as many as 50 percent of the Hispanic students for two grades and 25 percent for three grades (Moore and Pachon, 1985). It is clearly apparent why students from groups sharing significant elements of this profile, including those from poor white families, have been termed "at-risk" groups. Unfortunately, communication distance and problems of at-risk students with respect to middle-class groups and the schooling experience are expected to intensify, due in part to the marginalization effects of differences in income, class, and language. Examples of factors leading to this anticipated intensification are presented in the following section.

   Minority population and income patterns & intergroup relations. The population of poor and minority groups is increasing rapidly through immigration, higher than average birth rates, and the extension of poverty. European immigration to the United States in 1985, for example, accounted for 13 percent of the 570,000 new immigrants, while Asian and Hispanic accounted for 46 and 37 percent, respectively (Bouvier and Gardner, 1986).[3] Immigration, even more than fertility, is perceived as needing to be stemmed as a means to control U.S. population growth. Recent surveys have indicated, for example, that respondents favor placing restrictions on immigration and that the percentage of respondents who favor such action is increasing (Bouvier and Gardner, 1986). Thus, as the population of minority groups increases, negative attitudes toward their presence become numerically greater.

   Members of minority groups are a younger population group than nonminority group members. The mean age of Mexican Americans, for example, in 1980 was twenty-three, while that of the country at large was thirty (Davis, Haub and Willette, 1983). By 1985, although the average age of Mexican Americans remained virtually stable (23.3), that of the total U.S. population had risen to 31.9 (Arias, 1986). The population of minority groups also increases due to immigration, both legal and illegal, and immigrants tend to be younger than the average in the U.S. population. The mean age discrepancy, then, between minority groups in general and that of the nonminority population is widening. Thus, the proportion of minority students in schools is increasingly greater than their proportion of the total U.S. population.

   Minority group members also compose a significant percentage of U.S. families who are designated as "young families," that is, those headed by a twenty to twenty-four-year-old. Poverty within this category is increasing both in terms of declining income and number of families designated as poor. Young families, for example, have experienced a 27.4 percent decline in earnings between 1973 and 1986, while the income for all families experienced a one percent decrease (Commission on Work, Family and Citizenship, 1988).

The gap between the median income generated by households headed by young families and that generated by all U.S. families has widened over the past two decades (1967–1986). Young families in 1986 earned 52 percent of the median income earned by all U.S. families, or 32 percent less than they did in 1967 (ibid.). Within the young families category, income loss was especially great among blacks (46.7 percent), but also substantial among single-parent, female-headed households (32.4 percent), white non-Hispanic (19.4 percent), and Hispanic (18.5 percent) families (ibid.).

Unemployment within this category is also high: 6.8 percent for whites, 11.0 percent for Hispanics, and 20.3 percent for blacks (ibid.). In the U.S., then, poverty is increasing among young families, both in terms of numbers of families in the category and with respect to the income that they generate.

Under the above dismal socioeconomic conditions, it is no surprise that educational progress has declined for blue-collar minority families. From 1976 to 1985, for example, the proportion of black student enrolling in college has declined from 34 percent to 25 percent, while that of Hispanic students has declined from 36 percent to 27 percent (William T. Grant Foundation, 1988). Although reports consistently stress metropolitan/urban socioeconomic and educational statistics, conditions in rural America are even worse for blacks and Hispanics, as well as for poor whites (O'Hare, 1988).

Segregation of language minority groups: a profile of the Hispanic in the United States. Segregation, whether along minority racial or ethnic lines, remains rampant in U.S. schools. For the Hispanic student, however, segregation since 1954 has actually increased (Arias, 1986). This phenomenon is especially alarming as Hispanics comprise the single largest ethnic and language minority group in the United States, and, together with the native American, the one with the earliest historical presence. Most people labelled "Hispanic" in the U.S.—some 60 percent of the seventeen to twenty million—are of Mexican origin, while Puerto Ricans, Cubans, Central and South Americans account for the remaining 40 percent.[4] Over the past three decades, the effects of various demographic, social and economic factors have combined to form a profile of Hispanics which is not merely highly visible but also of major national concern.

Hispanics continue to have the highest cumulative immigration flow (legal and undocumented) into the United States, the highest population growth and birth rates, the youngest people, and the lowest skill levels and median incomes (cf. Borjas and Tienda, 1987; Davis, Haub, and Willette, 1983) of any other immigrant or native group in the United States. Their annual birth rate of 2.2 percent, for example, is the highest in the United States, and almost three times that of the total U.S. population (Oxford-Carpenter, 1984). Although the Hispanic family is significantly larger than the average white family, their median family income is 70 percent that of the median income for white families and their poverty figures (24 percent) nearly three times greater (Davis, Haub, and Willette, 1983). Moreover, not only were there no income gains for Hispanic families during the decade 1970–1980, but the proportion of Hispanic families who live in poverty has continued to increase (Moore and Pachon, 1985). Therefore, their numbers and their socioeconomic plight are increasing at a rapidly disproportionate rate compared to the total U.S. population.

Hispanics: race, ethnicity and education. Hispanics as a group are considered members of the Caucasoid division of the human species. This term, more popularly termed "Caucasian," is a racial classification which, in the United States, is considered "white." The term also includes people of northern European ancestry, but, more generally, "groups of peoples indigenous to or inhabitants of Europe, northern Africa, southwestern Asia, and the Indian subcontinent, and peoples of this ancestry in other parts of the world" (*The American Heritage Dictionary, Second College Edition*, 1985, p. 249). More specifically, however, Hispanics tend to be of European-Indian ancestry (Connor, 1985), although there remain, to lesser degrees, Indians and Europeans, as well as other groups (e.g., Asians, blacks) and blends representing the above racial classifications.

Historically, this predominantly Spanish-Indian racial blend has served, in the United States, to make ambiguous the racial and ethnic status of Hispanics. Furthermore, this dualism—that is, the racial classification of "white" with physical characteristics generally unreflective of the Anglo-Saxon notion of "white"—has served as a segregation device throughout U.S. Hispanic students' educational history. From a U.S. historical perspective, the racial status of the Hispanic became a legal question in 1897 when the United States denied Ricardo Rodriguez, a legal U.S. resident, naturalization status since he was considered neither black nor white, but rather of the "red," or Indian, race (Salinas, 1973). In *In re Rodriguez* (1897), the court determined that Rodriguez was indeed entitled to U.S. citizenship, even though anthropologically he "would probably not be classed as white" (Salinas, 1973, p. 390). Similar perceptions of the Hispanic's racial status have been used to segregate Hispanic students from their Anglo-Saxon counterparts throughout the present century, particularly in the southwestern and eastern states (Arias, 1986;

Barrera, 1979; Moore and Pachon, 1985; Wollenberg, 1978). Over the past three decades, segregation, rather than decreasing (as in the case of blacks), has increased for Hispanic students (Arias, 1986).

Ironically, although school systems have historically segregated the Hispanic from white schools due to perceived racial differences, there have been cases where Hispanics have been recognized as white in order to be grouped with blacks as a means to comply with court-ordered school desegregation mandates. In 1970, for example, sixteen years after the *Brown v. the Board of Education* decision, a Federal District judge held that Mexican American students in the Corpus Christi Independent School District had been segregated and that a dual system of education had been established which excluded both black and Mexican American students from their Anglo-Saxon counterparts. *Cisneros v. Corpus Christi Independent School District* represented the first case in which official recognition was given to the notion that, for purposes of desegregation, Mexican Americans were an "identifiable ethnic minority group" and entitled to the same protection as blacks were under the *Brown v. Board of Education* decision (Salinas, 1973, p. 366). This ruling was important since many Texas school districts had claimed that as Mexican Americans were white, they could be placed in schools with blacks in order to comply with the U.S. Supreme Court's desegregation ruling (M. Waldron, *The New York Times*, August 30, 1970, p. 68). Thus, members of two "disadvantaged minority" groups were being merged as a means to avoid integrating either with their Anglo-Saxon counterparts. Despite this and other favorable rulings (e.g., *Keyes v. School District No. 1*, 1973, cited in Zirkel and Richardson, 1988), segregation of Hispanics has, as previously mentioned, actually increased to the point that Hispanics are presently the most highly segregated group in the United States (Arias, 1986). Worse still, there is as yet no evidence of a national policy to desegregate Hispanic students (Orfield, 1986).

Integration policies, intergroup communication and educational outcomes since 1954. Research since the 1954 Supreme Court landmark decision has generally demonstrated that (1) physical integration does not in itself result in social integration, (2) academic performance among minority students has not significantly improved and continues to severely lag behind that of white, non-Hispanic students (e.g., Levin, 1985; Morris, 1979, pp. 759–764), and (3) feelings of inferiority have remained, as have anxiety and prejudice across racial and ethnic groups (e.g., Aronson and Osherow, 1980; Monti, 1986).

The problem of maintaining minority racial and ethnic groups in physical and social isolation from their generally more affluent Anglo-Saxon counterparts is compounded by a number of factors. Perhaps the most important factor is the increasing number of *de facto* segregated schools, most of which are in metropolitan areas where minority groups tend to reside with growing frequency.[5] Eighty-five percent of all Hispanics and 76 percent of all blacks reside in metropolitan areas, as compared to 66 percent of all Anglos. Schools also tend to reflect disproportionate representation (Navarro, 1986). Sixty-eight percent of all Hispanic students, for example, attend schools with a minority enrollment of 50 percent or more (Arias, 1986).

The phenomenon of segregation continues to occur for many reasons, including residential pattern differences associated with income and race or ethnicity (cf. Yinger, 1985), legislation which precludes transporting students to schools outside their neighborhoods, the Supreme Court's expressed respect for local judicial autonomy in desegregation matters, and the relative value attributed by political administrations to federal involvement in desegregation issues (cf. Astik, 1988, pp. 144–151; Salomone, 1986, pp. 42–72). Thus, the need for reducing social barriers and for promoting and implementing effective and positive communication skills among students within a heterogeneous learning context is complemented and complicated by the seemingly paradoxical, yet parallel need for nonsegregated U.S. schools. This latter issue is far from resolved as arguments by ranking federal spokespersons reflecting separate-but-equal positions (e.g., W.B. Reynolds, 1986) are articulated alongside arguments by integrationists (e.g., Tatel, Lanigan, & Sneed, 1986), leading one analyst (Orfield, 1986, p. 92) to conclude that more than thirty years after the *Brown* decision "there is no political or intellectual consensus about where we are, what we have learned, or where we should be going in moving toward equal education for minority children in American public schools." Consequently, movement toward desegregation remains plodding and essentially by dint of law.

Given the virtual historical lack of experience in meaningful integration across U.S. school systems for racial-minority and language-minority children, the question regarding the quality of current and prospective integration experiences must also be addressed. We do not suggest that integration as a product has an additive identity, rather that, as a process, integration must necessarily gain a critical mass in order that social relationships among students, teachers, administrators, and parents within the educational setting be significantly altered vis-a-vis one another. Thus far, however, we have suggested that the process of integration is not foreseen as gaining this critical mass in the near future. Therefore, acknowledging beforehand the limitations and necessity of an additive perspective, a representative review of the extant literature on social relationships, especially between student peers, should enable us to generate some preliminary implications regarding what educators and researchers might realistically expect in the type of heterogeneous classrooms currently available. Thus, we now explore those instances where racial/ethnic integration has physically occurred and the social and academic outcomes which have ensued.

Student relationships in the heterogeneous classroom. Desegregation success appears to be intimately linked with class as well as race. Monti (1986), drawing from his case-study analysis of the St. Louis (Missouri) Mandatory Voluntary Metropolitan Desegregation Plan, together with evidence and conclusions arrived at by other researchers (Crain et al., 1982; Hochschild, 1985; Orfield, 1985), affirms that (1) desegregation practices, when implemented poorly, can actually worsen race relations between and among economically mixed racial groups; (2) researchers tend to perceive successful desegregation experiences, whether real or conjectured, as characterized by homogeneity across significant variables such as class, financial stability and family stability, and by heterogeneity relative only to race; (3) desegregation practices involving mixed socioeconomic status students of different races can be successful if the lower-income blacks represent only a small number of students in an otherwise predominantly white, middle-class, larger school setting; (4) large-scale desegregation will not work where socioeconomic class status across students, regardless of racial designation, represents different levels; and, (5) the least financial needy school districts (i.e., white, middle class) receive the greatest funding, while the most financially needy school districts (black, low-income) receive the least.

Among the most dismal statistics which Monti cites, however, relate to how the money received is spent, and to black and white student attrition rates. Less than 5 percent of the $23 million received by the districts from the State of Missouri between 1982 and 1985, for example, was used toward "legitimate desegregation-related costs" (p. 58). Attrition rates within a two-year period in these districts were predictably high: slightly higher than 40 percent for blacks and 50 percent for whites.

Finally, the relative impact on students, both black and white, must be considered. In its fifth year (1985–86), the St. Louis program enrolled 541 white and 7,126 black students. Not only is there a glaring disproportion of whites (7 percent) to blacks (93 percent), but also an insignificant number of the total county student population participating in the public school desegregation program. Monti (1986) concludes that the St. Louis program "demonstrates that most minority children will remain confined to segregated and poorly funded schools and have their problems overlooked even when a highly regarded metropolitan desegregated order is in effect" (p. 62). There is a general consensus, moreover, that important aspects of Monti's conclusion (i.e., segregation, insufficient funding) character- ize the plight of minority students throughout U.S. minority-domi- nated schools (Orfield, 1986, p. 93). Disagreement continues, how- ever, among researchers and those who make and influence educa- tional policy, with regard to the various ways in which to characterize, measure, explain, and resolve the debilitating effects of educational inequality associated with current segregation practices (Orfield, 1986).

Surprisingly, the variable of school inequality has had only an ambiguous association with general societal racial and ethnic ine- quality (together with class and gender) in the controversy regarding segregated schools and minority educational problems in general (Kinder, 1986; Klineberg, 1986; McCarthy, 1988; Sniderman and Tetlock, 1986). Racial inequality has remained at the fringes of the theoretical constructs developed by both mainstream and radical educational researchers (McCarthy, 1988). There is evidence that what researchers find and the way they choose to express and interpret those findings may be influenced by racial biases. McCarthy (1988, p. 266), to illustrate the use of coded white discriminatory rhetoric, for example, cites references regarding the use of embedded code words and phrases such as "overcrowding," "welfare mothers," "the lack of experience" and "strain on current resources" in reports. There are other, less subtle, examples of ambiguously discriminatory practices which are applied to minority groups. Gann and Duignan (1986), for example, employ language that appears to blend coded discriminatory rhetoric with overt discriminatory rhetoric through- out their nearly 400-page publication on Hispanics in the United States, a singular modern achievement that is an affront to objective scholarship. In explaining poor academic performance and high drop out rates among Hispanic students, Gann and Duignan (1986, p. 234) write: "Moreover, a high percentage of illegitimacy, concubinage, and abandoned mothers and children among Hispanic slum dwellers created a poor environment for learning and staying at school." The authors compound their flagrant violation of objective scholarship with slipshod documentation, placing reference numbers at the end of such statements to imply that they furnish supporting or clarifying sources. In the above case, however, all that is provided to substantiate the authors' claims regarding percentages of "illegitimacy," "concubinage," "abandoned mothers and children" and "Hispanic slum dwellers," are various educational performance statistics on students from the 1971 Report of the U.S. Commission on Civil Rights and 1980 U.S. Census (Gann and Duignan, 1986, p. 353).

Other researchers (e.g., Fordham, 1988; Matute-Bianchi, 1986) have conducted investigations within urban areas having similar socioeconomic and racial/ethnic profiles, and have presented their findings within a traditional scholarly framework, judicious in language code, with the text supported by pertinent references. Under these circumstances, the content and communication style work together to promote understanding of the complex factors underlying achievement, underachievement and failure in school by minority students within the same urban area, even the same school. The schooling experience for minority students in urban areas begins to take on an aura of stressful complex richness, a blend of psychosocial factors that are culturally incompatible and which need constant, conscious balancing. Some minority students handle the demands of the schooling experience better than others. Some see what is required for academic success and embrace it; others see it and reject it. The consequences of either accepting or rejecting the schooling experience can be a severe risk; in short, academic success for the minority student can be as devastating as severe underachievement or failing. Research in this tradition contributes potentially powerful explanatory models of academic achievement among urban minority students and also suggests further research, without disparaging, however subtly, the students or their sociocultural milieu.

Fordham's (1988) research, for example, addresses a conflict emanating from the fictive-kinship-induced cultural demands placed upon black urban students clashing with the mainstream cultural demands made of them by the school. Fordham posits that this conflict between the collective social identity expressed within the black community and the spirit of individualism valued by white mainstream society, and the ambivalence which ensues, produces complex coping strategies on the part of black students. Two, mutually exclusive, strategies which black students use in attempting to resolve this cultural ambivalence are characterized by rejecting the schooling achievement ethic or accepting it totally. Those students who attempt to reproduce their culture within the school, tend toward failure and underachievement; those who adopt the school's culture, tend to sacrifice their own, becoming "raceless" as a means to avoid the wider community's sanctions for being black, and thereby increase their chances to succeed in school and, later, achieve vertical social mobility.

The role of color, Fordham suggests, is a predominant feature within the black schooling experience and students tend to be well aware of the social stigma of being darker in their shades of pigmentation and of the bitter social conflict and social artifice it produces when interacting within white society or its socialization institutions. Thus, to avoid both cultural and racial stigmata associated with things black, high-achieving, raceless black students tend to forsake not only their home and community culture, but their association with physical blackness as well.

The communicative effects of raceless behavior in intraracial and interracial interactions are also complex. They often result, on the one hand, in subordinating the verbal expression of one's true feelings in order to maintain the illusion of agreement with his or her white counterpart and the illusion of distance from black people and culture. On the other hand, raceless communicative behavior maintains one's raceless identity and social distance within the black community through language use (e.g., only standard English) and attitudes (e.g., individualistic, competitive) toward his or her black classmates and others outside the school at the expense of the fictive kinship behaviors identified with their immediate black urban community. Fordham (1988) provides numerous examples of this phenomenon in her research and that of others (e.g., Campbell, 1982; Gray, 1985; Klose, 1984; Monroe, 1987; Morgan, 1985), and suggests that, although both high-achieving male and female black students successfully maintain a raceless persona, female students demonstrate a greater ability to assume a more consistent raceless personality than male students. Male students, she found, are more internally plagued by the conflicts borne of cultural ambivalence and their behavioral actions sometimes reflect the dynamics of this conflict, even to the point of denying themselves the full extent of their already enhanced educational opportunities for the sake of appearing normal to their black, less academically successful peers. Generally, however, both male and female black high-achieving students agree that academic success entails leaving behind one's black culture and adopting the values of the dominant culture. There appear to be disturbing effects, however, to his or her communicative interactions with black and white peers as a consequence of this decision.

In both the black male and female student experience, important, even fundamental, cooperative principles of communication (Grice, 1975) are violated in the pursuit and exercise of their raceless persona, in both intraracial and interracial interactions. The social and linguistic distance which they maintain within their racial group, for example, brings into question the *relevancy* (what is being said) and *manner* (how one says things; for example, the strict use of standard English with underachieving black peers) of their communicative initiations and responses (Grice, 1975). This distance is compounded by the physical distance imposed between high-achieving and their less-successful peers in the form of special classes (e.g., advanced placement classes), resulting in virtual segregation by achievement level. Likewise, the verbal subordination of their true feelings toward a speaker's comments in interracial interactions makes doubtful the *sincerity* or *quality* of their responses (Grice, 1975).

The net effect of this communicative behavior among high-achieving black students is two-fold: communicative interactions will not progress smoothly due to perceived irrelevancy and obscurity, or will be characterized by communicative artifice due to disguised sincerity for the sake of maintaining smooth progress. Thus, cooperation at the communicative level between groupings composed, on the one hand, of same-race minority students with different academic achievement levels and, on the other hand, of minority-majority students with high academic achievement levels, may well be threatened in classroom settings unless structured intervention is provided to promote meaningful communicative learning interactions and to avoid communicative segregation, breakdown and artifice.

Similar patterns of communicative segregation and breakdown to those described above for black students also exist within Hispanic student groups in their biracial and intraethnic communication, although intraethnic (i.e., Hispanic) divisions appear more diversified than those reported for black students. Matute-Bianchi (1986) found that success in high school among Hispanic students appeared strongly tied to adopting school and community (Anglo-Saxon) norms, role models, and expectations (e.g., higher education and well-paid employment), but unlike the raceless persona high-achieving black student syndrome described by Fordham (1988), not at the expense of the particular group's cultural milieu. Conversely, she found that failure tended to be associated with distancing oneself from those same dominant-group norms, role models, and expectations in favor of a castelike cultural behavior set which was local, societally marginal, economically limiting, and consciously antagonistic toward the dominant group.

In analyzing school success and failure of the Mexican-descent students, Matute-Bianchi eschewed the term *Hispanic*, finding that coping strategy sets differed markedly across five intraethnic socio-cultural groupings, namely, *Recent-Mexican-Immigrant* (RMI), *Mexican-oriented* (MO), *Mexican American* (MA), *Chicano* (C1), and *Cholo* (C2). The MO and MA groups tended to be consistently more success-ful in school achievement than the remaining three groups, but differed from each other with respect to the proficiency level and use of their first language (Spanish), the use of their second language (English) in and outside of school, the school clubs which they chose to join, and their perceived cultural identity. The Mexican-oriented students, for example, although generally fully proficient in English and Spanish, preferred to socialize within their Mexico-born peer clique, both informally and within school clubs virtually composed of proficient-Spanish speakers and saw themselves as *Mexicano* (sic). Students identifying themselves as Mexican American or Americans of Mexican descent generally were born in the United States, domi-nant in English, perceived by school staff to be totally assimilated within the mainstream (Anglo-Saxon) culture, and active within school clubs in which Anglo- and Japanese-American students par-ticipated.

The students within the *Chicano* group used various self-iden-tification labels (*Mexican, Mexicano, homeboy/homegirl, Chicano*), comprising as much as half of the total Mexican descent student population, were typically enrolled in general or remedial courses (i.e., not college preparatory courses), and generally fared poorly in school. This student group was consciously alienated from main-stream white peers, school activities, and their successfully achieving Mexican-oriented and Mexican American peers, who they saw as wishing to be Anglo-Saxon. Their alienation, and, consequently, categorical identity, were reinforced through identification with al-ternate cultural preferences in language, music, and dress. Moreover, their negative attitudes toward regularly attending school, bringing books to class, completing homework assignments, and classroom decorum, promoted school failure and intensified perceived and actual differences between Chicanos and the mainstream, MO, and MA student groups.

The *Cholo* group was found to be numerically insignificant, but highly visible because of their "obvious stylistic cultural symbols" (Matute-Bianchi, 1986, p. 240) and their perceived association or sympathy with gangs. Neither the MO or MA group identified with the label *Chicano* or *Cholo*, considering each as synonymous with the other, as well as offensive and dissociated from mainstream (middle class, upwardly mobile) behaviors and values. Both the *Chicano* and *Cholo* groups were held in low esteem by students from other Hispanic groups, by mainstream students, and by teachers, and perceived by all groups to be academically unsuccessful.

The last grouping, *Recent-Mexican-Immigrant*, was generally well-perceived by teachers, regardless of the students' degree of academic success, mainly due to their exhibited positive attitudes toward school and their comparatively high level of effort, politeness and pleasant demeanor within the school setting. Students within this group demonstrated different levels of Spanish-language proficiency, which essentially collapsed into those recent immigrants having the appropriate grade-level proficiency in Spanish and those who fell below grade-level proficiency. Academic success within this group was largely a function of first-language proficiency (Spanish), which, in turn, appeared to be largely a function of the level of school attainment in Mexico prior to immigration to the United States.

Thus, Matute-Bianchi found that Mexican-descent students are not monolithic in their socio-organizational structure within the school setting, exhibiting instead co-existing, but noninteracting, social organizations which promote within-group segregation and negative stereotypes toward one another. Meaningful within-group (i.e., Hispanic) cooperation or communication is, within this framework, greatly inhibited. Furthermore, the type of social organization grouping to which a particular Mexican-descent student belongs is strongly linked to various expressions, behaviors and outcomes which are ultimately school-related. These include:

(1) *intra/intergroup perceptions* (e.g., how a group sees itself; how others see it; how it sees others). Perceptions also extend to how faculty and staff perceive students within the various within-group (i.e., Hispanic) student categories;
(2) *symbols of cultural identity* (e.g., dress code, language use, kinesthetic behaviors);
(3) *the respective degrees of integration* with mainstream students and involvement with mainstream school-related activities; and, ultimately,
(4) *academic success.* (Matute-Bianchi, 1986, pp. 236-245)

Matute-Bianchi found, moreover, that Mexican-American students, like the Japanese-American students in her same study, appeared fully integrated, psychologically and physically, within the mainstream school setting. These students tended, for example, to join school clubs and activities that were commonly shared by mainstream students (e.g., United Nations Club). Mexican-oriented students, in contrast, although also successful in school, demonstrated their cultural distinctiveness and difference from their mainstream, Japanese-American, and Mexican-American peers by generally joining the **Sociedad Bilingüe**, a club which reinforced Mexican culture and social activities, as well as the scholarly development of its members. This reinforcement of a native culture within the structure of the school was conspicuously absent from the alternatives created or found by high-achieving raceless persona black students in Fordham's (1988) research mentioned earlier.

Interracial/interethnic contact, as we have argued, does not necessarily promote interracial/interethnic communication. And interracial/interethnic communication may not necessarily lead to interracial/interethnic transfer. Matute-Bianchi, for example, presented evidence that successful Mexican descent students were comparatively aimless with respect to the long-term consequences of their studies. They tended to associate academic success with having a good job and sufficient material possessions but did not actually identify a particular career field or specific profession within a field. Japanese Americans, on the other hand, tended to make a tangible link between studies in higher education and a definite profession (e.g., engineering, dentistry, law, medicine, pharmacology, education). Japanese Americans were also, unlike the successful Mexican-descent students, knowledgeable about the relative value accorded particular kinds of high school math, science, and English courses by colleges and universities and how these courses helped in competing for admission to those higher education institutions perceived as more prestigious.

Another example of nontransference gleaned from this study concerned formalizing avenues for nonmainstream cultural expression. Successful Mexican-oriented students, for example, tended to join the *Sociedad Bilingüe* to reinforce their perceived native language (Spanish) and culture (Mexico). Japanese Americans, in contrast, did not formally organize school activities to promote or display native Japanese cultural expressions.

Thus, the data and analysis presented by Matute-Bianchi strongly corroborate earlier and current conceptual developments supported by empirical evidence (e.g., Allport, 1954; Hallinan and Teixeira,

1987) that mere physical contact within the integrated school setting does not lead to broad communicative contact across racial and ethnic groups. Similarly, there was virtually no evidence that contexts within which interracial/interethnic communication might take place (e.g., mainstream school-related clubs where Mexican-American, Japanese-American, and Anglo-Saxon students participated) exert a crosscultural influence. Therefore, the values, perceptions, and behaviors of the respective racially and ethnically different student groups appear to remain intact and self-contained.

The composite picture which has developed, then, of integrated school settings within today's urban and rural school contexts appears strongly characterized by separate, co-existing student groups, divided along inter/intraracial and inter/intraethnic lines, where academic success varies with respect to group orientation and where social and academic cooperation, communication, and influence across groups are minimal. Given this complex social configuration within the integrated school setting, the issue has become one of identifying and implementing instructional alternatives through which racial, ethnic, social, and intellectual borders among students may be transcended to foster cooperation, communication, and a more evenly distributed pattern of academic success. Our next chapter presents and discusses one such instructional alternative currently visible within the classroom: cooperative learning.

Notes

1. Levin (1985) describes the educationally disadvantaged as:

Persons from nonwhite, Hispanic and immigrant families, and from households where parents have low income and little education, [who therefore] tend to complete fewer years of schooling, are more likely to drop out of high school and show lower test scores in virtually all academic subjects than their more advantaged peers. (p. 3)

2. *Black Nationalism in America* (1970), edited by J.H. Bracey, A. Meier, and E. Rudwick, presents an especially interesting view of black alternatives, interpretations, and philosophies to segregated life within the United States. The book is a compilation of historical documents written by black leaders, intellectuals, scholars, and activists, dating from 1787 to the late 1960s.

3. Bouvier and Gardner (1986) also point out that Asians "far outstrip" immigrants from Spanish-speaking countries in terms of educational, occupational status and income. Bouvier and Gardner also expect that the Asian

immigrant will assimilate into the U.S. mainstream but that Hispanics thus far have exhibited a preference for preserving their culture and language.

4. We have been using the term "Hispanic" to embrace the different groups which all trace their backgrounds to a Spanish-language country. This term, while powerful in that it has apparently enabled more numerically accurate census data (see Davis et al, 1983), tends to blur the socio-cultural-economic distinctions among the groups comprising the term. Mexican Americans, Puerto Ricans, Cubans, Spaniards, Central and South Americans (excluding in the two latter cases those from non-Spanish language countries) each have group patterns that are not shared by one or more of the other groups. In the United States, for example, while the Hispanic median age is twenty-three (vs. thirty for the total United States), Cubans' median age is forty-one. Similarly, Cubans' income is higher than all other Hispanic subgroups.

5. The following definitions, adapted from O'Hare (1988), apply to the terms *metropolitan*, *urban*, and *rural*. Metropolitan refers to an area comprised of counties which surround cities of 50,000 or more inhabitants. It implies a socioeconomic linkage between peripheral counties and a core county. *Urban* refers both to (1) large cities and their heavily populated, neighboring suburbs and (2) any place having a population of at least 2,500 people, irrespective of location. *Rural* refers to any area not labeled as urban.

Cooperative Learning within
the Integrated Classroom

Integrated Learning Contexts and Group Relations

Contact theory and practice: inter-group and intra-group coop-eration among students in integrated instructional settings. Current approaches to organizing and delivering instruction within the integrated classroom are generally not conducive to establishing inter-group cooperation or communication (cf. Stephan and Brigham, 1985). Essentially, school settings value competition among all students "for grades, for teacher approval, for places on the student council, or on the cheerleading squad" (Slavin, 1985, p. 47). Communicative contact between diverse groups is also constrained by traditional classroom seating arrangements which separate students, teacher-centered instructional practices which discourage discourse between students, separate school-related social activities, and segregated transportation to and from school due to students' different neighborhood residential patterns (Slavin, 1985). These conditions tend to instructionally resegregate students within physically integrated school settings.

Resegregation is further nurtured within integrated school settings by grouping minority students on a between-class ("tracking") or within-class basis ("ability-grouping"), along assumed cultural, genetic or cognitive differences (Epstein, 1985). Thus, cooperation and communication among racially and ethnically different students within the same physical school environment are inhibited by classroom practices, which, in turn, can negatively effect students' achievement and motivation. Epstein (1985) presents an analysis of data originally gathered by the Educational Testing Service (ETS) in 1974 from 5284 students in the fifth grade, and 886 teachers, in ninety-four elementary schools in southern, northern, and western states. Teacher responses indicated that between-class tracking (54 percent) and within-class ability grouping (84 percent) remain prevalent and that tracking assignments were generally fixed throughout the students' elementary school experiences. Epstein also found that tracking and ability grouping were more likely to be used by teachers having negative attitudes toward integrated education, while teachers with positive attitudes toward integrated education were more likely to employ active learning and equal-status instruction. The latter type of instructional strategies, which incorporated multiethnic texts, biracial projects, discussions about race, and two-way cross-race peer tutoring (i.e., black tutors tutoring white students as well as white tutors tutoring black students), appeared to be positively associated with black students' achievement. Furthermore, based on student responses, grouping practices which enabled student movement across designated tracks (i.e., flexible tracking), promoted active learning (i.e., student responsibility for learning and behavior), or reflected equal-status programs, had significant positive effects on the achievement of black students. Compensatory education (i.e., pull-out programs), on the other hand, exerted a negative effect on white students' achievement, while the number of years which students had experienced integrated education positively affected the achievement of white and black students. In summary, although resegregative grouping practices prevail, it is the integrative grouping practices which are more likely to increase black students' achievement.

Thus, after nearly four decades, the criteria established by Allport (1954) with regard to effective integration of interracial groups remain minimally met within current integrated school settings. For example, the list of five criteria, presented by Rothbart and John (1985, p. 100) and attributed to Cook (1984), needed to achieve positive attitude change within the interracial contact setting continues to reflect Allport's (1954) earlier criteria:

a.   equal status among participants,
b.   individual attributes that successfully challenge the minority stereotype,
c.   mutual interdependence,
d.   promotion of individual perception, and
e.   promotion of egalitarian norms.

Rothbart and John (1985, p. 100) observe, moreover, that most contact settings in which blacks and whites interact violate the above criteria, thereby thwarting positive attitude changes at the interracial level. Epstein (1985, p. 24), differentiating between "true integration" and "mechanical segregation," extends the above list of criteria by adding the need for an educational environment where (f) the probability for success is high, (g) goals sought are commonly held, (h) tension, frustration, and conflict are lacking, and (i) a "natural proximity" exists among the different groups. Given the evidence presented in previous chapters (e.g., Fordham, 1988; Matute-Bianchi, 1986; Milk, 1980; Neves, 1984) with respect to the perceptions, status differences, and other features promoting segregation and noncommunication between academically more successful black and Mexican-descent students and their less-successful, same race/same ethnic group counterparts, these nine criteria appear both as necessary and as violated at the within-group level as at the interracial/ interethnic group level.

Slavin (1985) posits that cooperative learning theoretically satisfies the criteria for successful integrated experiences associated with Allport (1954) in that students participate across racial lines in group learning activities where cooperation, equal-status roles, and knowledge of each other as individuals, can develop in an integrated context purposely designed and actively supported by the classroom teacher. Slavin presents seven principal methods of cooperative learning which have been researched within integrated schools. Each of the seven methods offers, according to Slavin, practical educational advantages beyond promoting interracial/interethnic integration in that each is cost effective, relatively simple to implement, applicable across subject matter areas and grade levels, and does not require additional resources. More importantly, four of the seven cooperative learning methods have demonstrably improved students' achievement more than traditional instruction. The methods identified by Slavin (1985, pp. 49-50) are summarized below:

1. *Student Teams-Achievement Divisions (STAD).* Teacher presents a lesson, which is then studied collectively by students in four-member teams, heterogeneously grouped according to student ability, sex, and ethnicity. Students then take individual quizzes and team scores are tallied. Each team score reflects the degree to which the team has improved since its last quiz and is the sum of the difference between each member's current score and past highest score. Team scores are given visible recognition at the classroom level. Information regarding the development of this method may be found in Slavin (1978).

2. *Teams-Games-Tournament (TGT).* Equivalent to STAD in purpose and method, but uses academic game tournaments rather

than quizzes and improvement score approach. Teams having students at the same level of past performance compete with each other attempting to contribute to their respective team's score. Information regarding the development of this method may be found in DeVries and Slavin (1978).

3. *Team-Assisted Individualization (TAI)*. Students work at their own level and pace on individualized instruction elementary math in four-to-five-member heterogeneous teams. Each team has total responsibility for task completion, review, and management. The teacher works on similar concepts with a group composed of members from various teams. Each week, certificates are given to those teams who have achieved targeted levels of competence as evinced by the amount of units successfully completed by all team members. Information regarding this method may be found in Slavin, Leavey, and Madden (1984).

4. *Jigsaw and Jigsaw II*. The original version of Jigsaw teamed six students heterogeneously, with each member being designated an "expert" responsible for a specific part of particular assignment. Each expert gets together with experts from other teams having the same responsibility in order to discuss the material. Each expert then returns to their particular team to share the information for which they have responsibility. Thus, each of the six team members in fact teaches the remaining five members a particular information segment of the total assignment. Quizzes covering the total assignment are then taken by each team member, who receive individual grades with respect to their performance. Jigsaw II adapted the original version to the three other methods delineated above. Thus, groups are generally smaller and scores reflect team improvement gains. For example, each student now reads the same material but is responsible for learning a particular aspect of it. Discussions take place in expert groups and are then presented to the other team members. Individual quizzes are administered and scores tallied to form a team score. Team recognition is visibly acknowledged at the classroom level. Information regarding the development of these two methods can be found in Aronson, Blaney, Stephan, Sikes, and Snapp (1978) and Slavin (1980), respectively.

5. *Johnson methods*. Students work in small, heterogeneous groups to resolve activities on a common worksheet. Members receive praise and rewards as a group. Slavin points out that these methods are the "least complex" and "closest to a pure cooperative model," in that neither competitive nor individualistic ele-

ments are integrated. While this observation is valid within the particular research study which Slavin cites (i.e., Johnson and Johnson, 1981), complexity in the form of cooperative group structure and concrete instructional strategies has been fundamental to their substantial body of research (see, for example, Johnson, Johnson, Holubec and Roy, 1988).

6. *Group investigation.* Teams of two to six members, self-selected by the students, divide a classwide learning unit into different segments. Each team is responsible for a particular segment and each individual member within the team is responsible for a specific part of that segment. Segments are integrated and presented as a group project. The project is evaluated on its quality. Further information regarding the development of this method may be found in Sharan and Sharan (1976).

7. *Weigel et al. methods.* This method reflects the use of a combination of cooperative-learning strategies revolving around heterogeneous groupings. Evaluation and awards are based upon the quality of the group project. This method is based upon a study conducted by Weigel et al. (1975) involving a large number of white, black, and Hispanic students in junior and senior high schools over an extended period of time.

The above methods have been applied in numerous studies, however, Slavin (1985) specifically reviewed nineteen experimental studies, which met criteria associated with rigorous research, including length of study (minimum three weeks; median, ten weeks), appropriate use of research methods and analyses, number of subjects (minimum fifty; median, 164), and percentage of minority students involved (range: 10 to 61 percent). Each study focused on the effects of cooperative-learning methods on intergroup friendship patterns within integrated school environments. Slavin points out that sixteen of the nineteen studies (84 percent) demonstrate that friendship patterns, albeit to varying extents, improve between interracial/ interethnic students when principles of contact theory as articulated by Allport (1954) are met.

Friendship patterns, it is interesting to note, can be defined as one-way and two-way, and occur only in specific settings within the school. With respect to the former point, Weigel et al. (1975), for example, found that white students' attitudes toward Mexican Americans improved, but not attitudes of whites toward blacks, blacks toward whites, Hispanics toward blacks, or Hispanics toward whites. Thus, a one-way improvement (a nonreciprocal relationship) in attitude, while a measurably significant improvement from a statistical perspective, may not significantly improve in social interaction terms a physically integrated/socially segregated school setting where intergroup attitudes generally remain barriers to improved communication and interaction.

Friendship patterns may be characterized as two-way (a reciprocal relationship), yet be limited to only particular contexts in the larger school setting. Johnson and Johnson's (1981) research illustrates this point by providing evidence that interaction between racially different students was greater within cooperative classes than within individualized classes, but only during free time.

In summary, based on evidence provided by experimental research of comparative rigor, interracial/interethnic communication and interaction may be enhanced by cooperative learning methods, but the outcomes (in this case, friendship patterns) may (a) leave some, or even most, groups attitudinally or behaviorally unaffected by the cooperative learning experience, (b) manifest themselves only within certain contexts rather than throughout the general school day activities or where the teacher would desire to have them occur, and (c) depend on the particular cooperative method used. Prediction of improved and reciprocated friendship patterns, based on interracial/interethnic activities within the framework of cooperative learning, therefore, remains complex and uncertain.

Slavin (1985) also addresses ways in which cooperative learning affects other dimensions of contact theory, specifically the strength of friendship choices and the effects of (a) perceived and situational equal status between partners, (b) perceived similarities between partners, and (c) cooperative learning on extending interracial/interethnic friendships beyond the members within the particular cooperative learning groups. Slavin feels that cooperative learning effectively addresses the dimension of conditions for contact based on a secondary analysis of his past research (Slavin, 1979) by Hansell and Slavin (1981) in which they found that students in the STAD group showed significantly more interracial friendship patterns of a close and reciprocated nature than did the control group. The term *close* was applied to names identified within the first six choices on each subject's list; no data were presented with respect to the range of total names submitted or their mean number.

In addressing the second dimension of contact theory, that is, the notion of equal status between partners, Slavin appears to equivocate in his attempt to counter a refinement to the term *equal status* by Cohen (1975) which includes a performative dimension. Cohen argued that within the same learning context, differential performance expectations on the part of the diverse ethnic or racial groups toward each other would operate. These differential performance expectations, moreover, would possibly override the equal status attributed to everyone by virtue of being enrolled within the same class. This latter notion emphasized situational equal status (Cook, 1969), which, according to Slavin, meshes with Allport's (1954) perception that all people within the same situation would gain an equal status which would neutralize racial status differences.

Slavin then generates the awkward assumption that if white students did in fact perceive black students as less competent, as Cohen suggested, the white students, when working together in a cooperative activity with black students, should identify them as being less liked. Based on this assumption, evidence is then presented (Slavin and Oickle, 1981) to demonstrate that white students actually improved their friendship patterns toward black students when placed within a cooperative learning context. It is important to note, however, that black students did not improve their friendship patterns toward white students. Thus, Slavin (1981, 1985) argues that the presence of one-way, nonreciprocal relationships as reported on self-report sociometric indices contradicts the possibility that Cohen's performative notion of unequal status is operating within integrated educational settings. Notwithstanding this stance, Slavin concedes that cooperative learning research has not yet "measured status perceptions" (p. 56) and that future research in this area could substantiate Cohen's notion.

There is a more fundamental problem with Slavin's equal status argument than the development of questionable assumptions and equivocating positions, one which concerns the interpretation of Allport's message regarding equal status among racially different groups. According to Allport (1954), the issue of status revolved around changing the negative and misinformed perception held toward black males by white males within a common working situation. Specifically, in a heterogeneous grouping (e.g., racially and/or ethnically diverse) characterized by elements of prejudice, equal status is achieved through a process in which the minority group members, *already equal* in skill level to their majority member counterparts, are *perceived as being unequal*, and in the process of striving toward a common goal demonstrate their equalness, which subsequently leads to a positive change in the white males' perceptions toward their black co-workers. It is this combination of *comparable skill levels coupled with the appropriate cooperative context in which to demonstrate them that leads to perceived equal status among racially/ethnically diverse group members.* Thus, the situational context, by itself, is hardly sufficient to accord perceived equal status to groupings composed of racially or ethnically diverse students. This is especially true given, as Slavin (1985) points out, that classrooms in general stress competitiveness and individuality rather than cooperativeness. There appears, therefore, no ground for the interpretation Slavin derives from Allport's (1954) work:

> In Allport's use of the term, students in the same grade level have equal status, regardless of race, sex, or achievement level. Allport was concerned more with occupational status...than with status associated with ascribed characteristics or abilities. This kind of equal status is referred to by Cook (1969) as "situational equal status." (Slavin, 1985, p. 55)

Slavin also acknowledges that research is lacking with regard to two other major dimensions of contact theory: institutional support for cooperative learning, and perceived commonalities among peers within the cooperative learning setting. The need for institutional support was articulated by Allport (1954) due to the perceived friction associated with, and uniqueness of, equal status working relationships among racially diverse employees:

1. *Leadership, Friction Reduction, Policy Setting*
   To hire Negroes with minimum friction it seems advisable for management to lead the way in breaking down discrimination at the top level. Likewise a firm policy ruling will probably offset the initial protests that are likely to occur. (Allport, 1954, p. 263)
2. *Institutionalizing Integration Policies and Practices*
   In short, equal-status contact may lead to a dissociated, or highly specific, attitude, and may not affect the individual's customary perceptions and habits. (Allport, 1954, p. 264)

Thus, extending Allport's notions of effective contact to educational sites (e.g., at federal, state, county, district, school and classroom levels), institutions and management must take a long-term leadership role in setting concrete policies and engaging in visible practices that actively and articulately demonstrate integration. Slavin's (1985) interpretation of Allport's message, however, places significantly less direct responsibility on school management and socialization agents for spearheading the integration process:

teachers and administrators are often quite uncomfortable about the issue of race, being unsure whether race should simply be ignored ("We're all the same here") or whether race relations should be openly discussed and dealt with. Students may get the idea that while racial conflicts are not permitted in school, positive cross-racial contacts are not really encouraged. One simple change that cooperative-learning methods may make in the desegregated classroom is to clearly legitimize positive interracial contact...This climate may be created without speaking a word about race....(p. 57)

Finally, with respect to perceived commonalities, Slavin (1985, p. 57) posits that each racial and ethnic grouping carries with it important differences in values, as well as in socioeconomic status and preference for particular types of activities, that maintain their separateness from other racial and ethnic groups. To Slavin, these types of dissimilarities are difficult to overcome within the desegregated classroom and are a significant factor in friendship patterns maintaining a same-race/same-ethnicity profile. Slavin suggests that the relatively common cooperative learning practice of having team membership comprised along heterogeneous lines, such as race or ethnicity, will give the members a common identity: "Cooperative learning provides each student with a group based less on ethnicity or sex than on shared goals; the mere announcement of group assignments begins to break down racial barriers to friendship as students perceive their shared identity" (p. 58).

The above conclusion reflects the notion of situational equal status which, as we have illustrated, does not readily correspond to Allport's (1954) or Cohen's (1975) performance-based notion of attaining equal status. The conclusion also is not borne out by Slavin's own research (Slavin and Oickle, 1981) in which white students' friendship patterns toward black students were not reciprocated.

In summary, the cooperative learning methods embodied in the nineteen studies reviewed by Slavin (1985) only partially address the salient criteria delineated by Allport nearly four decades ago. Two basic points resulting from our analysis of Slavin's (1985) review are of especial interest in understanding how cooperative learning methods thus far have facilitated socioacademic integration among racially and/or ethnically diverse students.

First, evidence remains scant that meaningful integration, especially as measured by reciprocated friendship patterns, has resulted from the application of these methods among different racial or ethnic groups within the same physical learning context. Our analysis of Slavin's review, moreover, supports the notion that social integration among students from different racial and ethnic groups will not generally occur solely as a result of the specified cooperative learning methods. Other studies, moreover, indicate that cooperative learning effects among heterogeneous groupings vary with respect to the type of cooperative learning method utilized and whether or not the cooperative task was successfully accomplished. Miller, Brewer, and Edwards (1985), for example, cite research which suggests that (1) competition between cooperatively structured teams neutralizes some of the positive gains made through cooperation at the intrateam level (Johnson, Johnson, & Maruyama, 1984; Kagan, Zahn, Widaman, Schwarzwald, & Tyrell, 1985; Sharan, 1980), and (2) cooperative assignments resulting in task failure can diminish intergroup appeal (Worchel & Norvell, 1980; Worchel, Andreoli, & Folger, 1977).

Second, the variables of equal status and institutional support clearly warrant continued investigative refinement. The notions and respective influence of situational and performative status, and those of direct and indirect support policies and practices, on integration efforts within the schools demand clarification and assessment.

In light of these points, then, a patent need remains for research designs whose methodologies incorporate both qualitative and quantitative components to more ably and amply capture, analyze, interrelate and interpret those student and teacher behaviors within the physically integrated cooperative-learning classroom. Meaningful integration at the school level, as opposed to the classroom level, it must be stressed, is not solely a function of a particular set of interrelated behaviors within a classroom. These types of cooperative behaviors, as clearly stated by Allport (1954), must characterize the relationships between and among administrators, staff, teachers, parents and students within the total school setting. It is this complex of behaviors which, depending on the relative degree to which the principles of integration are collectively adhered to by the participants, leads to or constrains the equitable socioacademic integration and achievement of racially and ethnically diverse students, first within the same classroom learning context, and later, or perhaps concomitantly, within the larger structural school setting, and ultimately, within mainstream U.S. society.

It is therefore imperative to underscore that physical proximity, a common curriculum, and cooperatively-based learning methods, while necessary, are in themselves not sufficient to change exclusionary attitudes based on race or ethnicity to inclusionary ones. Thus, to actually effect such worthy and essential educational states, we must also appreciate and integrate the role and influence of particular intergroup dynamics common to contact situations. These include an appreciation of the complexity and strength of attitudes and expectations with which racially and/or ethnically diverse student groups (and teachers) enter the physically integrated classroom setting. We must also remain cognizant that integrated groups of co-workers experiencing favorable cross-race/cross-ethnic attitude changes toward one another within the confines of a particular setting do not necessarily transfer such favorable attitudes to other members of the different race or ethnic group within the wider institutional or community context.

Thus, questions remain with respect to the extent that cooperative learning settings can change segregated behaviors to integrative ones and the extent to which those integrative behaviors which do occur can be effectively transferred to contact situations outside the classroom. Recent works regarding interracial/interethnic contact situations from the perspectives of cognitive processing, intergroup anxiety, and category-based social interactions, address these salient questions. First, they describe elements which negatively affect intergroup interactions and how they operate with school settings. Second, they present preliminary social interaction models which may override these negative behaviors and lead to more socially integrative behaviors. Although each of the three areas is presented discretely, there is actually considerable conceptual overlap since the areas all reflect issues within contact theory and cooperative learning as these relate to interracial/interethnic educational settings.

Cognitive-processing. A summary of Rothbart and John's (1985) cognitive-processing model lends insight to the dynamics, difficulty, and limitations of attitude change within interracial contact settings. First, if a belief is to change, it must be susceptible to change and, if so, must be disconfirmed as a result of the contact. Certain stereotypic traits, however, are less susceptible to disconfirmation than others. Rothbart and John point out, for example, that although easily observable ascribed traits such as "messy," "neat," "quiet" and "talkative" are more prone to disconfirmation, groups in conflict tend to ascribe less observable traits to one another such as "untrustworthy" and "devious," which are less subject to disconfirmation. They suggest, moreover, that unfavorable traits are the easiest to acquire and the most difficult to relinquish, while favorable traits are the most difficult to acquire and the easiest to relinquish. Additionally, Rothbart and John point to the relativeness and complexity inherent to the notion of disconfirmation. Specifically, they propose that the occurrence of disconfirmation depends on three factors: (1) the degree to which an experience is clearly and specifically contrary to an existing opposing belief, (2) the number of behavioral instances involved in the disconfirming process, and (3) the number of contact settings allowing for disconfirming behaviors (Rothbart & John, 1985, p. 83).

Another important element within the Rothbart and John cognitive processing model concerns how individuals choose to categorize disconfirming behaviors. Individuals establish mental categories within which are stored and retrieved attributes respecting others. The placement of attributes within categories, moreover, reflects a dynamic process in which the individual determines which attributes will enter, remain within, or be deleted from a particular category.

Thus, a black or Hispanic professional might disconfirm a particular stereotype associated with blacks or Hispanics, yet the holder of the stereotype may categorize either professional within an alternate (subordinate) category (e.g., by profession) which *excludes race or ethnicity* rather than within a superordinate category (e.g., black, Hispanic) which *combines race or ethnicity with the disconfirming behavior*. In this way, the stereotype remains intact. In effect, *the less stereotypic the minority group member's attributes, the easier it is to maintain the stereotype toward the minority group at large*. Within this model of cognitive processing, the atypical reinforces the typical. Studies which we reviewed in the previous chapter provide corroborating evidence for this tendency: Fordham (1988), for example, in her description of school personnel who mentally and socially represent successful black students in a raceless manner, as well as Matute-Bianchi (1986) in her depiction of teachers having favorable or unfavorable views toward Mexican-descent students in relation to their perceptions of students' cultural proximity or distance, respectively, to Mexico. As Rothbart and John point out, transference of the perceived positive but atypical attributes from the individual to the group is difficult, as neither is identified with the other in the mental categorizations of the holder.

The actual process by which attitude change occurs is not well understood. However, Rothbart and John speculate that change is a function of the diminished predictive utility of a stereotypic category coupled with a shift toward more specific categorizations of a minority individual's behaviors. That is, the goodness-of-fit between events viewed and predetermined expectations, which enabled the stereotype to operate successfully, is continually challenged by disconfirming events contrary to the stereotype. Under these conditions, the belief holder adjusts the major (stereotypic) category to store the contrary evidence as well, and through this movement from fixed to variable data storage, diminshes the predictability of the data stored and, by extension, the general utility of the stereotype. Rothbart and John caution that this admittedly speculative and optimistic process of change would hold only if the predictive value of the stereotype were susceptible to disconfirmation and if the relative incidence of stereotypic confirming behaviors, however slight, did not override the disconfirming behaviors. Ultimately, the authors are considerably less sanguine regarding the possibility for positive attitude change within the present social framework:

> Although we would like to be optimistic about the possibility of change, it seems more realistic to conclude that the conditions leading to change through contact are quite restricted...[I]f one considers the typical contact settings in which, say, blacks and whites interact,...most violate all of...[the stated] conditions necessary for favorable attitude change. In other words, in a society where there is enormous social inequality between groups and many behavioral differences associated with that inequality, it is extremely difficult to satisfy...the conditions outlined here. (p. 100)

Intergroup anxiety. Intergroup anxiety is another factor which can inhibit effective communication and behavior between students from diverse racial or ethnic backgrounds. Stephan and Stephan (1985) propose a model in which intergroup anxiety is created by three sets of factors: (1) the amount and conditions of prior intergroup contact, (2) the type and degree of intergroup cognitions, and (3) situational factors. Intergroup cognitions comprise feelings toward the outgroup which are based on "knowledge of the outgroup, stereotypes, prejudice, expectations, and perceptions of dissimilarity" (p. 158), as well as upon feelings of ethnocentrism; situational factors relate to the "amount of structure, type of interdependence, group composition, and relative status" (p. 158) comprising the particular contact setting. These sets of factors, in turn, can singly and in combination affect the behaviors, cognitions, and affective reactions of all of the participants within the contact setting. Members of racially/ethnically diverse groups may fear, for example, that working together on common activities can lead to negative psychological (e.g., loss of self-esteem) and/or behavioral (e.g., fear of domination) consequences, as well as negative evaluations (e.g., rejection) by members within each of the diverse groups (Stephan and Stephan, 1985).

The net effect of intergroup anxiety on interracial/interethnic relations is negative. A complex array of behaviors is set in motion within the contact setting which reflects to varying degrees the fears described immediately above. Rather than cooperation, then, the contact setting may produce anxiety-induced behaviors such as avoidance, exaggerated adherence and expression of in-group norms vis-a-vis the outgroup, and selective processing of social information reinforcing biases toward outgroup members, among others (cf. Stephan and Stephan, 1985). And, rather than the contact setting leading to modification of previously held negative attitudes, the interracial/interethnic contact situation characterized by elements of intergroup anxiety can instead reinforce existing biases that one group holds toward the other.

The social consequences of these anxiety-weighted contact settings can be antithetical to cooperative learning goals. Thus, interracial/interethnic structured group activities, rather than leading to the conceptual and behavioral changes indicative of a successfully integrated, cooperative-learning classroom setting, may well result in precisely the types of behaviors practiced by students in the research we have covered such as avoidance, communicative artifice, one-way friendship patterns, or other socially segregative behaviors.

Category-based intergroup relations. Miller et al. (1985) distinguish between category-based intergroup relations and personalized interactions within desegregated settings. They assume that personalized interactions are more likely to generalize to settings outside the particular intergroup context because these type of interactions result in attitude shifts which deter members of one group from identifying members of another group solely by category. Thus, through personalized interactions, the saliency of stereotypic characteristics will diminish in favor of individual characteristics. This process, if successful, would ultimately lead one to look at members from diverse racial or ethnic groups as individuals rather than as interchangeable human units reflecting a particular category. Under these conditions, one set of simplistic category identifiers (e.g., skin color or other differentiating physical characteristics) would not elicit a related category set (e.g., poor, uneducated, etc.), rather each member of the group would communicate and otherwise interact with all other members based on individual perceptions and behaviors.

According to Miller et al. (1985), however, the typical desegregated school setting contains features that favor category-based social interactions. Distinctions among students in these settings, for example, are strongly marked along racial/ethnic, class, culture, language, and status lines. Students are further differentiated from one another by political and educational policies which reinforce their identification as representatives of a particular social category with the school setting. Also, the present numerical imbalance between majority and minority students within the desegregated school is cited as a factor which encourages highly visible and emotionally strong identification with a particular category. The impact of these types of category-based elements on interracial/interethnic relationships promoted by cooperative-learning endeavors is overwhelming. According to Miller et al., to the extent that cooperative teams consist of members selected on the basis of category, cooperative intervention gains at the social level will be ephemeral at best.

Personalized interactions, then, are seen by the authors as the necessary ingredient within intergroup interactions which will effectively decrease category-based attitudes and behaviors and lead to interactions at the individual level. Miller et al. propose that task orientation within cooperative interactions be secondary to interpersonal orientation, and that assignments to teams or roles not be perceived as being made on the basis of an individual's category identity. The authors cite Teams-Games-Tournament (TGT) as an example of a cooperative-learning task that promotes category-based rather than personalized interactions. Cooperative teams, for example, are organized to reflect the ethnic and racial composition of the classroom ant then compete against each other for scores (see pages 53-54 for description of TGT). To Miller et al., category-based selection criteria for team membership and competition serve to hinder the social integration aim of the cooperative-interaction strategy through the heightened impersonalization and task orientation of the TGT cooperative-interaction strategy.

The authors present the findings of two studies (Rogers, 1982; Edwards, 1984) conducted within experimental settings at the university level which investigated the effects of category salience and task orientation on cooperative activities. The findings in both cases were consistent with Miller et al.'s paradigm in that bias was strongest against the out-group when category membership and task orientation were salient. Moreover, their evidence supports cooperative-learning activities which are noncompetitive and where team members are selected along real or ostensible individual criteria in order to enhance the quality of interaction among the students and the probability of generalizability to settings outside the particular classroom. Where competition remains a focus, even within cooperatively structured activities, the authors caution that it presents a threat to the positive quality and generalizability of the students' interracial/ interethnic interactions. The opposing team, for example, or even a within-group team member, can (1) be perceived as a threat to winning, (2) elicit feelings such as hostility and superiority toward others, (3) engender feelings of inferiority on the part of those members who feel, or who are made to feel, as if they are part of the out-group, and (4) reinforce negative stereotypes and status inequities. Under the above conditions, then, competitive and category-based selection practices are not likely to contribute to the aims of a socially integrated educational environment, even when complemented by a cooperative learning framework.

Conclusion. Returning to Allport's (1954) criteria regarding effective integrative settings, especially as rearticulated by Cook (1984) and Epstein (1985), and listed at the beginning of this chapter, we find that key principles associated with cooperative-learning methods generally, but not universally (e.g., TGT strategy), adhere to the conditions prescribed for effective interracial/interethnic contact settings. Johnson et al. (1984, 1988) probably offer the single best synthesis to date of the salient elements within cooperative learning methods which promote effective intergroup interaction: (1) face-to-face interaction, (2) positive interdependence, (3) individual accountability for mastering the assigned material, and (4) training in interpersonal and small group skills. These four conditions, as we have seen, are necessary but not sufficient elements in achieving improved interracial/interethnic social relations and academic performance. There are other, quite formidable, constraints upon effective communication, positive interrelationships, and improved academic achievement among racially or ethnically diverse student groupings within a heterogeneous classroom setting. Such constraints include status inequities, lack of direct institutional support, stereotypic beliefs, intergroup anxiety, and type of cooperative-learning model used. These constraints, if not foreseen and effectively countered, can override even the most well-designed cooperative-learning endeavors and reinforce the present segregated and resegregated *status quo* within our schools. Therefore, cooperative-learning models must attend to these constraints if they are to lead to the successful social harmony and academic achievement we are seeking for all students.

Part II

Learning Theory and Computer-Integrated Instruction

Introduction to Part Two

The application of learning theory to computer-using classroom contexts in elementary and secondary schools has been an ambiguous endeavor since 1963, when computer-integrated instruction was formally initiated by Patrick Suppes' research at Stanford University. At one extreme, educators have perceived the computer to be so essentially different from its educational technology predecessors (e.g., chalk and blackboard, book, radio, television) as to merit its separate classification as an instrument of intellectual development. At the other extreme, computers are seen as but one more related branch in the logical evolution of the educational technology tree.

These distinct orientations have, in turn, influenced the perceived nature of the computer and how to best use it within instructional/learning contexts. Consequently, the above-mentioned differences are of fundamental importance to how educational computer applications are integrated into classroom activities. Where the computer is viewed as a unique instructional/learning entity, for example, the computer may well become the surrogate teacher or companion. The particular instructional/learning event between student and computer transpires within this self-contained context. In contrast, where the computer is perceived as an extension of prior classroom technological aids, the role of the teacher may remain paramount in controlling the instructional/learning event and the degree to which peers, teacher and computer are integrated within that event. Either context, theoretically, could house programs that were remedial or enriching in nature.

These two contrasting views continue to enjoy positions of prominence within computer-integrated education development circles, although arguably not in the exclusive sense of earlier years. Recently, alternative methods of integrating computers into the learning activities of students have surfaced in research projects and conceptual articles, if not in widespread use within classrooms. The following section addresses issues, practices and outcomes with respect to diverse computer-integrated learning models. The models we have chosen are perforce selective but, we trust, representative of historical and current perspectives and practices. Toward this end, and for purposes of clarity and continuity, we have divided our general discussion regarding computer-integrated instruction into three major subsections, each comprising a separate chapter: (1) an overview of early philosophical bases, (2) an analysis and critique of current practices, and (3) a critical view of computer applications within culturally heterogeneous learning settings.

4

Philosophical Bases of Computer-Integrated Instruction

The Early Philosopher-Practitioners[1]

Alfred Bork. Machine control of instruction is not a new phenomenon, value, or concern of this century (Cuban, 1986). Addressing this perennial issue in its modern-day guise, Bork (in Taylor, 1980) cautions against philosophical perceptions and practices that place total instructional control in the computer:

> A tendency to allow technology control is inherent in employing technological aids to education. This trend is a mistake; teaching aims and teaching purposes should always be at the forefront...the primary emphasis should be on what students are to learn and how you want to teach it...Pedagogy should take precedence over technology in all cases (p. 31)

Nevertheless, Bork, since the late 1970s, has been generally critical of traditional instructional practices, criticizing their excessive reliance on whole-class instruction, conservative textbooks, lecture methods, modelling the product of problem solving but not its process, teacher talk, and repetition.

The resultant model of computer-integrated instruction that Bork envisioned, although democratic, was computer-bound rather than socially and subordinately integrated into a teacher-student-peer interaction model. For Bork, the elements that bring excitement and value to instruction could be programmed into the computer, so that instruction as an *individualized* event could transpire. Not only was the value of *self-paced, individualized* instruction paramount, but *the provision of instruction by the computer was to compensate for the detached teaching model practiced in schools.* The computer, then, according to Bork (in Taylor, 1980), was to *humanize* education:

> A student who does not learn with a particular approach can be presented with alternate learning materials. The learning experience for each student can be unique, tailored to the needs, desires, and moods of that student...I see this individualization as a *humanization* of education. With the computer each student can have a unique learning experience. (p. 60)

In Bork's world, self-paced instruction translates into student control over instruction. The limitations inherent in this vision of course are that the benefits and role of social learning are reduced to that which has been programmed for use in the computer. The philosophical intent, then, is social learning by surrogate, a rather simplistic, yet prominent, notion which recurs all too frequently in computer-instructional models. The computer's role in instruction is seen somehow as greater than the sum of its parts and, even more incredibly, as independent of them.

Thus, in Bork's framework, knowing how to learn and what to teach are known quantities, and the successful synthesis of these two elements only entails an objective intermediary. Even if one could not accept the naivete of such an assumption, one might presuppose that teachers are educated to undertake the responsibility of matching learning styles with learning needs, however imperfectly. But in Borkian terms, teachers are part of the problem, not the solution. Computers, on the other hand, are viewed as "having no prejudices (in Bork, in Taylor, 1980, p. 64)," as well as the wherewithal to address the learning the learning needs of any and all students. Bork carries this naivete to its logical absurdity:

> We can expect more self-paced courses, more emphasis on mastery learning...we can expect more emphasis on *self-paced curricula*...adapted to individual students. The self-paced curriculum may lead to the final destruction of perhaps the single most sacred feature of American universities, the four-year degree. (p. 65)

The point of our critique is not, of course, that universities should or should not require a four-year degree, rather that Bork could leapfrog from where we are in terms of the limitations of our pedagogical expertise to resolving all learning problems and inequities through a computer armed with good graphics and a self-pacing mechanism. In the form of a corollary to Bork's model, we are presented with the "cognitive enhancement" fallacy so common in earlier periods with respect to the value of learning Latin; in this case, the belief that will enhance a student's cognitive abilities.

In summary, we might, only somewhat facetiously, allude to the Borkian model in terms of the legend of John Henry. The computer is perceived as the steam engine and the inevitable changes that it brings with it. In contrast, teachers, despite their individual virtues and strengths, are viewed collectively as an inefficient, although living, relic, ill-prepared to meet the enormity of the educational task needing to be accomplished. We propose, however, that it is not yet time to trade in the human mind nor the potential of socioacademic learning for the programmed alternative residing within the computer and the individualized-learning model Bork advocates.

Bork's more current writings (e.g., Bork, 1985) advocate small group instruction and teacher input into software program development, but do so in a pedagogically awkward manner. When referring to the perceived positive outcomes of collaborative learning at the computer, for example, Bork chooses to focus on spelling: "spelling errors were corrected almost instantaneously, with strong peer pressure to spell correctly exerted at the very instant at which the spelling problem occurred (1985, p. 272)." Aside from the pedagogically uninspiring emphasis on using computers to promote correct spelling, Bork, perhaps unwittingly, also illustrates how talk might well reinforce competitiveness and stress among peers under the guise of cooperative learning. Thus, the actual benefits associated with cooperative learning in a computer-integrated learning setting are not visible within Bork's later framework although the notion of peer collaboration, however misinterpreted, is present.

Bork also appears pedagogically off the mark when integrating teachers into his software program development process. Bork's view of successful teachers is limited in that they are primarily prized for their "intuitive" understanding of subject matter, students and learning processes (Bork, 1985, p. 268). This perspective influences how he incorporates teachers into his development process, collaborating with them to tap the known information each has of their subject-matter area, and to compile the types of questions and responses, both correct and incorrect, that students will produce within a particular content area. The notions, however, of "known information," and "correct and incorrect responses" reflect a highly traditional approach to teaching and learning that has not generally fostered the development of higher-order thinking skills in students, irrespective of grade level. A more meaningful professional collaboration between teachers and designers would actively engage successful teachers in helping to develop creative learning scenarios that would tap and develop these skills in students through computer-integrated-instructional software.

Bork's model of computer-integrated instruction continues to appear sketchy after more than a decade of software development experiences. The unfortunate educational repercussion is that Bork has failed to amass through these research and development experiences the qualitative elements necessary to present a cohesive educational philosophy, or even cogent arguments, with respect to computer-integrated instruction.

Patrick Suppes. The Suppes model is perhaps the single best example of a drill and practice program, in terms of quantity, quality and longevity. Since 1963, Suppes has developed computer-integrated instructional programs that are individualized and remedial, and which only marginally rely, if at all, on the presence of a teacher. The Suppes model presupposes that computer-integrated instruction will serve a complementary function to, rather than supplant, the teacher's daily instruction. To this end, students work for ten to fifteen minutes per-day-per-subject area at the computer, reviewing in drill and practice form what they have previously been exposed to in class. Suppes' model has been especially prevalent at schools where low-income, minority student enrollment is high.

With respect to the type of gains experienced by students in this computerized remedial program, Solomon (1987) reports that the within-grade level gains achieved by students who are initially below grade level still do not place them at entry-level grade norm by the beginning of the next academic year. For example, during the course of any one academic year, a sixth grade student performing below sixth grade norms generally will not reach the end-year sixth grade norms. Thus, at the beginning of that student's seventh grade year, he or she will still be below grade level. This observation agrees with those of Levin's (1985, 1989) with respect to the futility of compensatory programs as a means to enable low-income, minority students to attain academic parity with their advantaged peers.

The role of integration, cooperation, and communication within the Suppes model is decidedly nonexistent from a human interaction perspective. The students generally file into the computer laboratory at allotted times, sit at their designated locations, access their particular file, and work until it is time to stop. These remedial settings tend to be characterized by silence, perhaps punctuated by murmuring voices of students speaking softly to themselves. Teachers within these environments, when present, may be grading papers, talking with the computer laboratory specialist, or otherwise conducting tasks unrelated to the rote learning activities of their students. All task-related behaviors of each students, such as the time at which the drill began, number of problems attempted, number of problems correctly solved and level of difficulty are all managed and recorded by the computer system. Thus, at the practical level, if not theoretically, the teacher's role is reduced to one of presence.

As Suppes' model is admittedly drill and practice, as well as thoroughly individualized, there is little to be gained from evaluating it in terms of what it lacks (e.g., discovery orientation, social learning attributes, communicative devices, etc.). Furthermore, the computer's role in Suppes' model is uncomplicated in philosophy and practice: it is a tool which, relative to the narrow function it performs, reduces instructional time and produces modest student gains. In a word, it knows and functions reasonably well within its limitations. There are two areas, however, of possible contention. First, as Levin, Glass, and Meister (1984) have demonstrated, the cost of computer-integrated instruction of the drill and practice type is higher than noncomputer instructional alternatives such as peer tutoring. Second, there remains the larger, inevitably philosophical, question as to how effective drill and practice programs are in addressing the educational needs of low-income minority students.

Nevertheless, computers, irrespective of their instructional cost-benefit ratio, continue their cell-like reproduction within classrooms and will surely prevail over present-day objections of expense. Also, in the absence of empirically-based alternatives which can be replicated, educators and administrators will not be prone to forsake performance-proven drill and practice programs of the Suppes types. Thus, despite our severe reservations regarding its practice among minority students (see below), we agree with Cuban (1986) that drill and practice programs will continue to be relied upon until more imaginative ways of teaching with them are devised, accompanied by substantive alterations in school and classroom settings.

In this work, we have chosen to place emphasis upon the three elements of integration, cooperation, and communication, as a means to altering instructional settings to favor significant socioacademic achievement among all students in the heterogeneous classroom. Our framework, moreover, has especially focused upon alterations that would increase the socioacademic achievement opportunities of low-income, minority students, who are either less than fully proficient in English or nonwhite. Suppes (1980s) understood well the importance of verbal interaction, but only placed instructional and theoretical emphases in the context of human-computer interaction. To Suppes, language, as teaching, was an unconscious phenomenon, not understood by those who performed either well or poorly. The problem, then, was not technological but theoretical: computers had to be programmed to talk, listen, know and instruct in a structured manner that would enhance the learning experiences of the computer-using student. Importantly, Suppes' concern for enrichment-based learning appeared to solely focus on highly gifted students, while his remedial programs were geared to "disadvantaged students."

There is no doubt that these frameworks (e.e., Suppes' call for communicative machine-human interaction together with our own socioacademic model) are more structurally complex and their effects more difficult to gauge in traditional evaluative terms than a straightforward mechanistic approach as is computerized drill and practice. There is substantial direct and indirect support, (e.g., Levin et al., 1984; Solomon, 1987; see also section below on computerized remedial instruction) however, for not solely relying on remedial programs and for seeking alternative computer-integrated educational methods and associated philosophical frameworks within which to embrace them.

Thomas Dwyer. The writings of Dwyer (1974a, 1974b, 1975, 1976) juxtaposed social learning with individual learning more as a means to contrast the two concepts than to encourage their synthesis. Creativity was, for Dwyer, an individual act, while social knowledge was a result of formal education. While both were necessary for a person's growth, schooling tended, in Dwyer's model, to emphasize the transmission of known information, that is, social learning, at the expense of creativity, or individual learning.

Talk, in Dwyer's model, was associated with social learning and, as such, a phenomenon to be modified from its natural state to one prompting creative learning. During learning, human language, as viewed by Dwyer, was an inactive element, and a necessary evil which should occur minimally and indirectly in between lengthy pauses so as to permit learning-related activities to transpire. Moreover, human language, as an expression of social learning, would tend to obfuscate, while its artificial, undeveloped counterpart, computer language, would promote individual creativity (Dwyer, 1974b):

[T]he principle that some things are best left unsaid for a while is a universal one. Of course something has to replace English, and this is where both the kinesthetic and artificial language aspects of computing have fundamental value. English words are mixed in, but in a crisp, precise way that seems to ring sympathetic chimes in most children (and adults). (p. 110)

Language, then, as it might develop between peers, for even between an instructor and students, within a computerized-learning setting, is critiqued and devalued.

There are other, equally contestable, assumptions that Dwyer makes with regard to the educational enterprise. Teaching, for example, is viewed as a social activity, and, by implication, devoid of creativity. Computing, somehow, "magically" converts the unproductive teacher-student relationship into a creative process in which both the teacher and student partake. For Dwyer, the "great teacher" is the experience shared by both student and teacher at the computer. Teachers without computers, then, are devalued by Dwyer (1975), in the same manner as was language:

There is another use of computer-related technology...that is triggering originality and depth in student work, as well as such vital qualities as enthusiasm and zest, particularly in the area of "math" education...It is use of technology that works its magic by freeing teacher/student groups from the restricted drill in facts and formulas. Teacher and student become, instead, codiscoverers of truths. The methods they learn to use, and the results they obtain, display a freshness that suggests that they have personally discovered a secret that transcends the art of any one great teacher. Their secret, put simply, is to use computer technology to build an environment in which learning mathematics is both natural and exciting. (pp. 114-115)

It is important to note that the notion of computer-assisted instruction (CAI) was viewed by Dwyer in the same manner as was conventional teaching, that is, essentially a method that might lead to repertoire (i.e., transmitted) knowledge but certainly not to new knowledge (i.e., creativity).

To summarize Dwyer's belief, control of the learning process by the student in his or her pursuit of new knowledge is the ultimate goal of education. Social learning serves a knowledge transmittal function that, while necessary, is not akin to actually learning or being in control of one's learning. The teacher's role during the transmittal stage is to clarify, inspire, guide, and propel the student toward learning on his or her own. (Dwyer, 1974a, p. 92). Computing, specifically, programming, is viewed as the agent which enables students to gain control of their learning and revolutionize teacher-student relationships from naturally conflictive to naturally harmonious.

Seymour Papert. Papert is arguably the best known of the computer education philosopher-practitioners. His worldwide visibility is especially high due, in great part, to his international success as a gifted mathematician, popular writer-thinker, author of Mindstorms, software program developer, most notably, Logo, and computer-integrated education researcher and project activist. Papert also worked with Piaget for five years (1960-1964), which exerted a profound influence upon Papert's philosophical framework, grounded him in developmental psychology (more specifically, genetic epistemology, or the origin and growth of knowledge) and understandably targeted his research, development, and writing foci on children. Given this rather unique background, the question we raise relates to Papert's resultant framework of educational philosophy, especially in terms of comparing and contrasting its assumptions, justifications, and implications to the computer-integrated instructional philosophies of his peers mentioned earlier.

Papert's best-selling book on the potential of children's computing, *Mindstorms* (1980), will be used to frame our analysis, as the book is at once autobiographical and treatiselike, and, given its widespread popularity and numerous printings, the single best example of Papert's educational philosophy. Papert's passionate belief in the transformational value of computers is itself a function of his own very early rather absorbing relationship with things mechanical:

> *I fell in love with gears* [at two years of age]. This is something that cannot be reduced to purely "cognitive" terms. Something very personal happened, and one cannot assume that it would be repeated for other children in exactly the same form. My thesis could be summarized as: What the gears cannot do the computer might. The computer is the Proteus of machines. Its essence is its universality, its power to stimulate. Because it can take on a thousand forms and can serve a thousand functions, it can appeal to a thousand tastes. (Papert, *Mindstorms*, 1980, p. viii)

More specifically, the value of the computer, according to Papert, was its perceived ability to reduce math and science to manageable concepts to the masses (*Mindstorms*, 1980, p. 4). The computer would serve as *the tool of mass cultural transition*, taking us from math and science illiteracy to math and science literacy. It would, additionally, bridge all cultures, classes, and disciplines, and integrate all these together with enhanced knowledge of the self. To Papert, moreover, the computer was a weapon which challenged current knowledge regarding human's age-dependent knowledge acquisition. The lure of computers was perceived as such a strong, integrating force that humanists, not just engineers, would be drawn into their fold. The computer, in a word, for Papert was the solution. Where, then, lay the problem? Unfortunate in its simplicity but not inexplicable given the technologist perspective that Papert embodies, the problem is society: "But there is a world of difference between what computers can do and what society will choose to do with them. Society has many ways to resist fundamental and threatening change" (p. 5).

Assuming computer access were left unfettered within the schools, what would be the computer's function vis-a-vis the student? According to Papert (1980), the student would learn to program the computer, *and in so doing*, would also harness the power within the most advanced technological device available, as well as "establish intimate contact" with some of the deepest notions of science, math, and intellectual model building known (p. 5). The child, in a phrase, needed only to have exposure and access to the building blocks of knowledge and he or she would be able to manipulate them to learn new concepts and skills. Concepts and skills that were, by their nature, unrelated to age. Mathematical concepts, especially, would become as natural a part of each child's behavior as his or her first language.

Papert's (1980) computer vision was unequivocal with respect to the role schools would play in his proposed revolution:

I see the classroom as an artificial and inefficient learning environment that society has been forced to invent because its informal environments fail in certain essential learning domains, such as writing or grammar or school math. I believe that the computer presence will enable us to so modify the learning environment outside the classrooms that much if not all the knowledge schools presently try to teach with such pain and expense and such limited success will be learned...without organized instruction. This obviously implies that schools as we know them today will have no place in the future. (pp. 8–9)

As stated earlier, *Mindstorms* is a highly personal account, so much so that Papert chose to use his own self-perceived experiences in math, as a form of quasi-case study, to support his beliefs and any generalizations which might be made. His early infatuation with gears and the fact that he had used his body to imagine how they turned had left an indelible impression upon his thinking which was to surface in adulthood in another form. These early experiences became the impetus for developing the "Turtle," an object with which to think. While Papert claims that the Turtle is not a "panacea for all educational problems" (p. 11), he nevertheless asserts that it will serve as the model for all future objects with which to think. Thus, the Turtle, like computers, is seen by Papert as *the* transitional element for cultural revitalization on a mass scale.

Armed with the tool with which to begin programming, the next societal barrier to be scaled is that of access, especially given that Papert suggests utopian one-computer-per-student ratio. Papert's economic justification is simple: assume a total computer cost of $1,000 per student over the thirteen-year, K-12, schooling cycle, and then factor in either larger classes or a shorter schooling cycle, both Papert-assumed consequences of computer efficiencies, and the price is reduced below the initial investment. If one is to understand Papert's economic justification, one must also understand his philosophical perspective, which was, for all practical purposes, an article of faith.

Papert, despite any empirical or intellectual evidence sufficient to support his thesis, imbued computers with qualities that would transform whole societies. Thus, for Papert, the world became a choice of cultural orientation: computer culture versus noncomputer culture. In Papert's vision, only computer-culture societies would enable a child's intellectual development to go beyond the artificial stages (i.e., Piagetian-identified stages) resulting from the constraints imposed by life within noncomputer cultures.

Logo, as the programming language Papert codeveloped and advocated, was at one level the means by which children could activate the Turtle. On another level, however, it was the means through which children would learn how to think about thinking:

Even the simple Turtle work can open new opportunities for sharpening one's thinking about thinking: Programming the Turtle starts by making one reflect on how one does oneself what one would like the Turtle to do. Thus teaching the Turtle to act or to "think" can lead one to reflect on one's own actions and thinking. And as children move on, they program the computer to make more complex decisions and find themselves engaged in reflecting on more complex aspects of their own thinking. (p. 28)

Even the benefits of writing via a word-processing program were viewed by Papert as revolutionary in that they enable children to "become more like adults, indeed like advanced professionals" (p. 31). Children, moreover, would have a professional, adult-type relationship not only with the writings which they produced but also in relationship to themselves. This outcome, according to Papert, would conflict with "the many aspects of school whose effect, if not whose intent, is to "infantilize" the child" (p. 31).

Thus, if schooling advocates really want to be effective, they must discard their antiquated concepts and practices and embrace instead the Piagetian notion of learning without curriculum. In Papert's terms, this means supporting children as they build their personal intellectual structures as well as "changing the culture, planting new constructive elements in it and eliminating noxious one" (p. 32). BASIC programming, for example, is, to Papert, a noxious element yet ubiquitous due to "sluggish" and conservative elements within education and because teachers expect all but the most exceptional students to do poorly in math-related activities. Another noxious element Papert identifies is drill and practice programs which remain because they are easy for teachers to teach and for engineers to design.

Accordingly, Papert reduces the complexity of the educational problem, even in its computer aspects, to societal conservativism having permeated the institution of schooling. In like fashion, he reduces the complexity of the educational solution to private individuals who, owning computers, gain control of their personal and families' education and consequent intellectual development through home computer use. Papert even posits that thinking can be enhanced through children imitating the mechanical aspects of computer programming:

By deliberately learning to imitate mechanical thinking, the learner becomes able to articulate what mechanical thinking is and what it is not. The exercise can lead to greater confidence about the ability to choose a cognitive style that suits intellectual sophistication. By providing a very concrete, down-to-earth model...work with the computer can make it easier to understand that there is such a thing as a "style of thinking"...Thus

instead of inducing mechanical thinking, contact with computers could turn out to be the best conceivable antidote to it. (p. 27)

In the above passage, Papert exhibits the philosophical extremism that permeates *Mindstorms*, despite his occasional reader-di-
rected protestation of objectivity. Computers driven by Logo are the
universal elixir for societally induced educational problems. These
computers, for Papert, transform all input into knowledge. Thus, even
imitation of the mechanical leads to intellectual enlightenment and
creativity. By this state, it is difficult to discern whether Papert is
discussing philosophy or alchemy.

Papert proceeds to illustrate how one's intuitive manipulation of
the notion of circularity can be improved through grasping the notion
of polygonal equivalence. His position is firm with respect to educators
modifying their instructional notions of math, and presumably all
disciplines:

I am not suggesting that one more exercise will change your
intuition of circularity...I am suggesting that you keep this new
way of thinking in mind for awhile, looking for opportunities to
use it as you might look for opportunities to introduce a new
friend to old ones. And even then, I have no way of knowing
whether you *want* to change your intuition of circularity. But if
it is to change I think that the process I am suggesting here is the
best, perhaps the only, way whether it is adopted deliberately or
simply happens unconsciously. (p. 150)

Finally, Papert asserts that children need to think procedurally, as do
computer scientists in their programming activities, if they are to
overcome the conceptual barriers to learning math. In this way, not
only will students' phobia toward math disappear, but they will also
experience success in it, and integrate it into their daily lives because
it will make sense to them.

Papert's extremism has come full circle, so to speak: the true
educators are those who think as computer scientists, the true
learning tool is the computer, the true conceptual learning link is the
Turtle (i.e., the point of commonality between an individual's external
physical experience and internal intellectual experience), the true
language of learning with which to articulate that linkage is Logo, and
the true product of education is a structurally procedural thinker (i.e.,
where knowledge acquisition is modularized rather than confronted

as a whole; the concept is analogous to structured programming). To Papert, the above paradigm reflects learning within a natural context, where teachers and students, novices and experts work together in a physically and structurally flexible manner toward a common goal. If schools and teachers, then, could only adopt this paradigm, students' success in school would be assured.

The Papertian vision smacks of naivete but is indicative of Papert's approach to expressing how he understands and structures his universe in *Mindstorms*. The bicycle analogy Papert uses serves as an example of how he envisions learning; his point is essentially that teachers must focus on a structure (a bicycle) rather than on the psychology of manipulating that structure (riding a bicycle). Papert (1980) states that people can ride bicycles because the bicycle in motion is an inherently stable machine. He substantiates his argument by further stating that if a riderless bicycle were pushed down a steep plane, it would neither fall over nor stop due to its structure (i.e., "the geometrical construction of the front fork," p. 159) compensating with counterdirectional movements those movements which would tend to unbalance it. Thus, a rider must learn, not to balance a bike, but to not unbalance it. In short, "learning not to interfere" (p. 159). The proper study of learning for Papert, then, is not the learner (the incipient bicycle rider), but that structure (bicycle) which is the focus of his or her learning activity (bicycle riding). Thus, teachers must study math (to include whatever domain of it that the learner is attempting to learn), not the student, if they wish to understand how math operates, and consequently how to teach it. Successful teaching, as successful learning, is reduced to a simple principle: focus on the structure rather than the individual.

One, of course, would hardly argue that structural or environmental conditions would ever be such that the above theoretical contention regarding a riderless bicycle's motion and balance could actually become a regular occurrence. Still, one could imagine ideal conditions where the riderless bicycle, once set in motion, could perpetually maintain its balance and motion. In reality, however, there are winds, potholes, the human force and thrust exerted to put the bicycle in motion, the geometric construction of the bicycle, and other factors which will prevent the riderless bicycle from anything but a short, almost inevitably costly, and clumsily executed downhill venture. Even structurally, there are cost, resource, quality control, market, and design factors, among others, that constrain transferring what is ideally structurally possible to what is the actual structural outcome. Thus, although tens of millions of individuals in the United States ride bicycles, many do so wearing helmets as recognition that there are potential dangers associated with bicycle riding in the real world. Theory is always clashing with reality in less than ideal ways, yet Papert either simplistically critiques the less than ideal or fails to acknowledge it. In either case, the role that reality plays remains unintegrated theoretically. Papert's vision ultimately fails, then, in its attempt to portray convincingly the computer as a realistic alternative to teaching or learning, regardless of the nature of the setting (home, school, other).

The above practical extension to Papert's analogy serves to highlight what we consider to be his expository weakness: Papert presents his model as an ideal, applicable to all, rather than in relation to schools or other types of social-learning settings. His protestations and comments to the contrary lend but a thin veneer of objectivity to his educational model. Papert shows no faith in schools or in teachers nor, in his blanket disapproval, an understanding or consideration of the different schools of educational thought and practice. Yet, he idealizes computer scientists, Logo-programmed computers, and structured programming, presenting all three as model elements for future intellectual development, and, worse, as the present set of human and artificial resources from which we need to draw. He dichotomizes reality into precomputer and computer cultures, and associates only the latter with the potential for intellectual development breakthroughs due to structurally programmed thinking at the child level. His view of learning is individually oriented, except where the student and teacher are working as equals within a learning context. Thus, socio-human mentoring basks in its limelight. Language outside the computer has a role but mainly in that it serves to engage the children in their computer-related pursuits, especially their "debugging" activities. Society, presented as a collection of inefficient, individually harmful, institutions and their attendant bureaucracies, is seen by Papert as a barrier to realizing his model.

In sum, Papert's technologistic vision is not unlike Skinner's utopian vision:

> I knew, as all teachers know, that education was inadequately supported. That was perhaps not its own fault, but its outmoded techniques certainly were...I saw that this could not go on. But I also saw that educators themselves could not save the situ-

ation. The causes were too deep, too remote, they involved a new conception of man, compatible with our scientific knowledge, which would lead to a philosophy of education bearing some relation to educational practices. But to achieve this, education would have to abandon the technical limitations which it had imposed upon itself...Nothing short of the complete revision of a culture would suffice. (Skinner, *Walden Two*, 259–260)

And, while at times lambently thought-provoking, Papert's model is ultimately a one-dimensionally contrived model of individualized learning, where elements from a student's natural context are suspended and supplanted by an idealized computer language serving as tool, tutor and tutee in the instructional/learning process (see Taylor, 1980). This model, moreover, is heavily dependent upon, and at the same time weakened by, the presupposition that neither human language nor instructional practices will enable the students to transcend their present intellectual limitations (e.g., how they perceive math; the sequence of age-dependent development stages through which they pass) and that the Logo-programmed computer will enable the students to do so.

Summary

Ultimately, the above philosopher-practitioners generally advocate structural changes in education in order to enable students and, only secondarily, teachers to realize their optimum potential and power within the constraints of a classroom. (Only Suppes' remedial programs are an exception to this perspective.) This goal continues to be worthy of pursuit. Nevertheless, the crucial, magical role in the largely self-paced, individualized learning process which they envision for computing, and programming in particular, remains off-target. Nearly three decades after Suppes initiated educational computing at the elementary and secondary school levels, computers and programming are no closer to offering us this technological panacea than they previously were at the level of public education.

In sharp contrast, the well-established research of investigators such as Allport, Cohen, and the Johnsons has contributed significantly to understanding how to establish positive, social contexts where students can work, produce, and achieve together as equals. Other investigators such as Matute-Bianchi and Fordham have contributed toward a better understanding of the complexities of intraracial and intraethnic student behavior and values that effect educational outcomes. These lines of qualitative and quantitative inquiry (all of which have been addressed in earlier chapters) contrast sharply with the obvious biases and unfounded assumptions plaguing the work of most early and, as we shall see, far too many current technologists. Johnson, Johnson and Holubec (1986) have stated with respect to cooperative learning that there is nothing magical in its innovation or its implementation:

> cooperative learning requires face-to-face interaction among students. There is no magic in positive interdependence in and of itself. It is the interaction patterns and verbal exchange among students promoted by the positive interdependence that affect education outcomes. (p. 8)

Their point, as we understand it, has implications for analyzing the computer education models developed or advocated by philosopher-practitioners such as Bork, Dwyer, Suppes, and Papert. First, cooperative learning celebrates that harmonious integration of the array of contextual and behavioral elements within a classroom in order that all students might benefit through active participation in the learning process. Second, it is an innovative means to address a persistently elusive, two-fold societal need: (1) to democratize educational opportunity through interracial and socioculturally integrative instructional practices, and (2) to enable language and other minority students to achieve parity in academic performance and average years if successful schooling vis-a-vis their mainly white, middle-class counterparts. Buttressing these theoretical and philosophical structures are burgeoning methods and techniques which help to operationalize the integration of student diversity and enhance collective and individual performance. Finally, the educational paradigm of cooperative learning is regularly subjected to and refined by qualitative and quantitative studies, many of which are empirically rigorous (e.g., Kagan, 1986; Slavin, 1985).

This type of development process has been traditionally lacking in discovery-oriented computer-integrated education philosophies. As we have seen, rhetoric and bias, at worse, and naivete, at best, have tended to inform their general pedagogical premises and direction. Technologists addressing educational issues must shed their mantle of romantic, magical computer notions in favor of disciplined inquiry. The degree to which this need is currently being met is the subject of our next chapter.

5

An Analysis and Critique
of Current Practices

Franz and Papert's "Computer as Material" Model

Description. The Franz and Papert (1988) model exemplifies how important social interaction and talk can be in the learning process, especially within a student-centered, authentic discovery-oriented learning setting. Yet, Franz and Papert merely describe incidents within the discovery process which involve talk between and among peers, as well as between the students and their teacher, rather than integrate its role in the learning process or address its value as a communicative tool which extends the discovery process beyond the self. Instead, they give priority to highlighting the methods and stages involved in the creative manipulation by the students of the material elements which ultimately lead to diverse material products, all of which could in one form or another measure time.

Within this context, they contend, the Logo-programmed computer offered advantages of precision, adjustment, adaptability and integration which extended the learning process in ways that the other materials could not. Thus, the authors' learning paradigm seems to suffer from myopia in that a crucial component within the learning process was not within their range of vision. In fact, their focus upon student interaction and talk appears blurred in the article as the following sequence illustrates:

1. Students introduced to notion that time must be measured through an empty glass jar being placed over lit candle,
2. Students' watches were collected and they were asked to predict at what point candle would extinguish,
3. "There was much discussion concerning different methods of

timing and the accuracy of each, prompting the students to
defend, evaluate, compare, and evolve their individual timing
systems" (p. 409),

4. Rock and classical music were played as students were involved
    in applying their personal timing systems and, on following
    days, students were asked to predict from memory the time at
    which the candle would extinguish,

5. "Discussion led to the conclusion that the rate of their body
    timers varied from one day to the next and that they were also
    affected by what went on in the class, such as the type of music
    that was played" (p. 410),

6. The need for creating a more precise timing mechanism was
    apparent and "[d]ifferent suggestions were offered...After a
    period of discussion, the teacher suggested that this was enough
    talk" (p. 410) and the time had come to actually build some
    clocks,

7. "While some students were speaking the language of Logo in
    order to achieve their goal of making a timer, others were
    speaking the language of a chisel, or of a battery and electric
    motor, or of a ball rolling down an inclined plane. What was
    important was that the students were learning to speak the
    languages of many different materials in the classroom in an
    attempt to create their clocks from ideas in their minds" (p. 411),

8. When the students had created mechanisms that produced
    consistent units of time, the teacher posed the question regard-
    ing how the different time indicators compared with the stan-
    dard units of seconds,

9. As the students encountered difficulty in discovering how to
    aptly relate these nonstandard units of time to the standard unit
    of a second, the following occurred: "A suggestion that spurred
    more fruitful directions of inquiry was the idea of thinking in
    terms of series of cycles rather than individual cycles" (p. 412),

10. "At some point, the students who were building Logo clocks
    realized that they could use their clocks in conjunction with the
    electric eye as timers for these Logomobile races. Now, different
    groups of students were working together, combining and ex-
    panding upon each others' projects" (p. 413),

11. "The point of these explorations is that different groups of
    students had come together to solve problems in which they were
    interested..They had all joined in a rather informal way and had
    worked toward a common goal" (p. 414).

Critique of the Franz and Papert model. The type of instructional/learning model which Franz and Papert illustrate appears weak on two counts. First, they trivialize the role of the computer as a medium for learning by labeling it a "material," and placing it within the same category as "test tubes, pulleys,...microscopes...scrap wood, broken electronic devices, marbles, and the like" (p. 409). The computer, its attendant software, both prepackaged and student-generated, and associated peripherals such as printers and drives, remain an expensive and elusive learning alternative proposition for schools. The benefit of added accuracy and coupling to other compatible devices (i.e., legomobile, temperature sensor), while interesting, do little to justify the cost or illustrate the creative use of such equipment in the classroom relative to other science activities which offer precision development and project extension opportunities. Their model is further constrained by the role relegated to discussion among student peers and between the students and their teacher in the instructional/learning process. As markedly visible in the above sequence (i.e., steps 1-11, above), talk exerted a major influence in the instructional/learning process, both formally and informally. It was especially crucial in enabling the students to capitalize upon a suggested alternative that they had not been able to conceptualize alone (see step 8).

Franz and Papert align themselves philosophically with Piaget and Dewey, among others, pointing out that their emphasis, like that of their predecessors, is on the inquiry and the learner rather than on the particular curriculum or set of facts to be learned. They offer painfully little, philosophically or otherwise, beyond a science-oriented activity for junior high school students which involves the use of a Logo-programmed computer in conjunction with other project-related materials. In previous chapters we have discussed the nature of integration, cooperation and communication, singly and in combination with each other, among heterogeneous student groups within the same learning context. These factors continue to interrelate and influence the learning process in classroom contexts where computers are present. Given this background, the outcomes presented by Franz and Papert leave critical questions unanswered, including (a) the homogeneity or heterogeneity along racial, ethnic, gender, and socioeconomic lines of the students, (b) the degree to which all students participated in the activities, verbally and otherwise, and (c) the types of discussion which ensued between student peers and between students and their teacher within the course of the science activities.

With this information we could discern the degree to which the setting were cooperatively oriented (i.e., inclusionary) rather than competitively structured (i.e., exclusionary), and how the nature of the discussions served to stimulate or curtail discovery-oriented dialogues among the students in general as well as within particular sets of student groupings. Also, the computer's role in the learning process from the vantage point of student discussions and other types of social interactions within this setting could be analyzed using this broader communicative framework.

There is yet one more concern with the approach advocated by Franz and Papert which has to do with the issue of equity. In earlier writings (DeVillar, 1986; DeVillar and Faltis, 1987), we discussed computer equity within the framework of student access, participation and benefit, citing evidence that these factors are influenced by ethnicity, gender and wealth. We also indicated that within industrialized countries information is projected to become a new form of wealth and computer/computing knowledge and information access are a new criterion for developing wealth. Thus, schools that do not provide comparable access to computers to all students sustain a system of social stratification that benefits some at the expense of others. In the type of context depicted by Franz and Papert, computer access, participation and benefit would appear to be a result of serendipity rather than purpose, thus favoring those students who gravitated toward the computer option. While using the other materials available within the science class could result in similar (or even enhanced) performance results relative to the activities pursued, those students not gravitating toward the computer would remain on the fringe of using it in a meaningful manner within this learning context. Thus, ironically, similar or even enhanced performance results might occur within a context of technological inequity. Therefore, if equity is to be actively sought at the classroom level, it is imperative that educators meaningfully integrate the computer into the curricular activities of all students whenever there are computers present. This principle seems especially applicable within the discovery-oriented, materials-diverse, learning setting described by Franz and Papert.

Nix's "Computer as Production Studio" Model

Description. Nix (1988) contends that contemporary educational practices involving computers have tended to establish a hierarchy between the student and computer where the former is subservient to the latter. The key to the computer's superiority over the student lies in the power derived from its programming relative to both content mastery and ways of acquiring knowledge, coupled with the institutional sanction the computer receives as the model for determining successful and unsuccessful learning. Thus, learning is reduced to known content and known paths to mastering that content. In short, knowledge and knowledge acquisition are relegated to the realm of the predictable. The consequences associated with this paradigm can be severe at both the societal and individual level. Nix (1988), for example, warns that the first practice leads to "mediocrity of knowledge" while the second poses a "threat to the dignity of the learner" (p. 419). Nix asserts that drill and practice programs, characterized by "prepackaged...relatively simplistic" (p. 419) information, not only reinforce the message that knowledge is predictable but also imply a strong association among learning the notions of right and wrong and the unambiguous application of these notions.

Drill and practice and tutorial computer programs, while perhaps the most obvious in their manipulation of the student, are not the sole barrier to creative learning. Any program that restricts students to a particular mode of problem solving or that builds in responses to cover the variability of learning styles across students, regardless of their sophistication, threatens creative learning and human dignity. Nix includes Logo, artificial intelligence (AI), and intelligent computer-assisted instruction (ICAI) as inhibiting learning in that the computer in each case presumes to know what or how the student is to learn. In the case of Logo, for example, Nix points out that:

> The problem-solving technique is computeristic. The domain of expression is defined basically in conceptual schemes related to computers, such as algorithmic thinking, procedural thinking, logical debugging, and modularization. Supporters of this type of role for the child at the computer define an important aspect of success in terms of the child's becoming an active problem solver of the type described. An ideal is for the child to master and become proficient at this type of creativity and problem solving in a wide range of domains beyond the specific computer setting that fosters it. It is at this processing level of predictability that the computer knows what the child will do. (p. 420)

Nix is apprehensive that these types of educational computer-using practices are detrimental to students' learning through creative processes of which the computer is unaware, and, to the degree that the students are constrained to only those methods of learning that are possible through the computer's program, not recognized as valid learning strategies. Under these conditions, the self-expression of the student in the learning process is severely curtailed and actively discouraged. This context, as stated earlier, can result in the mediocrity of knowledge and pose a threat to the dignity of the students. His plea, then, is for using the computer to its maximum advantage as a tool to enhance exploratory, rather than predictable, learning, in order that the aforementioned hierarchical relationship change from machine/program dominance to human-driven. Thus, the threats to exceptionality of knowledge (i.e., discovery-oriented knowledge) and human dignity (i.e., user-controlled knowledge acquisition strategies) posed by the computer-as-knower model at both the content and content-delivery levels will have been virtually eliminated.

Although admittedly in the initial stages of development, Nix provides numerous examples of how this alternative paradigm, termed *Making a Scene*, successfully worked for children in grades three, four, five, eight, and ten, from one school in New York City and a school district in Tarrytown, New York. From these examples, we appreciate that Nix's learning model focuses on the principles of student self-expression, creativity, and control of the learning process and tools within that process.

The students first learn a particular type of program (Handy) which uses English in a special, yet comparatively simple, way and which allows them to "construct interactive scenes presented on a computer" (p. 422). The computer, according to Nix, is an integral, but decentralized element within the *Making a Scene* learning context. The first reason is because the computer does not and cannot know what the children will produce or how they will produce it; thus, the element of knowledge predictability is eliminated in favor of student self-expression and creativity. Second, the computer is complemented by an array of electronic accessories which includes "video disc, video tape, synthesized voice, digitized voice, touch panel, animation, and graphics" (pp. 422–423), all of which can be integrated through the Handy-programmable computer to construct, present, and even operate a particular student-generated product. The product, moreover, is plastic in that it can be controlled and modified at any point by the student. The overall goal of the *Making a Scene* event, then, is to promote learning through creative self-expression using multi-media electronic devices to produce, present, and manipulate a product.

For Nix, learning is both creative and functional, and transcends the tools used to achieve and express it. From the point of view of the student, for example, learning is an enjoyable, unpredictable event that integrates various elements within the learning context which can be freely manipulated as the student's creative senses or comprehension of the product dictate. From the point of view of the school, the above endeavor has a specific purpose and outcome which can be assessed, and social and cognitive processes which can be adduced to have transpired as a result of the student's product.

Computers and the other electronic components are important to the learning process but do not control it. Nix offers the following examples of social and cognitive processes experienced, first, by fourth graders editing selected parts of a feature film (*Ghostbusters*) to create a humorous pitch for their school library, and, second, by tenth graders selecting video tape footage from *The Video Encyclopedia of the 20th Century* to create mock political campaign advertisements:

1.   [T]he child has to study the movie; analyze it; reconceptualize it; create a mode of presentation, including a mode of interaction for the intended audience; plan and create the objects; and write, try out, and revise the script. The creativity involved in doing this is not circumscribed by computeristic concepts. It involves a wider range of issues, many of which are "real world" issues that are unrelated to computers, such as humor, satire, and a challenge to authority. (p. 425)

2.   In creating the essays, a number of decisions had to be made by the students. Examples include: demographics of intended audience; relevance of the ad for the overall campaign; emphasis (record of achievement, personal qualities, platform, positive versus negative campaigning, and others); emotional tone; thematic integration; use of media (camera angles, based on what is available, sound, voice-over, annotation, graphics, and others). The students implement their decisions by creating objects consisting of text and pictures and other types of information, and writing a script to put it all together. (p. 426)

Critique of the Nix model. The model of learning that Nix provides us is not so much "computer-decentered" as it is comprehensively electronic. This latter description of course places the computer within a physical context comprised of other electronic media, all of which are in a production-type setting available to the students. From this perspective, the computer's role and electronic control are theoretically decentralized. Nix also emphasizes that the students' dignity remains intact, or is at least not threatened, by their ability to create and manipulate this electronic studio in accordance with their desires. No element within the electronic studio knows what the students are going to produce nor can it assess what is being or has been produced. Computer omniscience within the learning setting is eliminated at the same time that student expression and creativity are celebrated.

Along with the positive elements of student dignity within, and student control of, the learning process, the electronic workshop also brings with it serious problems as a viable universal learning alternative within everyday classroom contexts. Two obvious ones are cost and equity. The admittedly rhetorical nature of the questions we pose with respect to cost and equity does not diminish their relevancy: (a) How many schools can afford such sophisticated equipment and the expertise that goes along with operating, integrating, and maintaining it, physically as well as educationally?; and, (b) Assuming its presence, how many students within a school could gain physical access to an electronic studio on at least a weekly basis in order to participate meaningfully in electronically-driven project development activities and derive an educational benefit from them?

Another concern we share reflects the excessive two-dimensionality of this learning context. All learning is directed at producing scenes that reflect, even mimic, television, specifically game shows, newscasts, and commercial programming (e.g., "soap," "sitcoms," etc.). The ultimate focus is the production, intended to be presented as a product on a flat screen, which when measured diagonally, may be likened to a television screen. Audience effect, camera angles, lighting, sound, takes and retakes, qualitative and quantitative compromises due to time, actors, scripts, etc. all reflect life within the two-dimensional mold of movies, videos, and television. It is obvious that this model might not be appropriate for many individuals. Also, given its dependence on a learning context essentially based on constructing a sequence of images to entertain or educate an audience through a two-dimensional medium, its ability to sustain students' interest as producers and as viewers over longer periods of time is suspect.

There are, moreover, other concerns which must be addressed. How are these experiences different, say, from those already lived by thousands of theater or studio arts students? Have these latter types of students experienced intellectual development significantly different from those students not exposed to this type of academic experience? Do they have, for instance, a heightened sense of integration, cooperation and communication which enables them to work effectively and democratically within heterogeneous groupings? Again, these questions lean inevitably toward the rhetorical.

Wherein lies the difference, then? What are the *Making a Scene* students doing differently that other students in the past and present do not have access to? In essence, the difference lies in that they are manipulating Handy, the software language, to integrate and control their comprehensively equipped media learning setting. This difference is costly and narrow in scope (i.e., electronic workshop), and hardly justifies its expense relative to other learning alternatives that provide at least comparable learning experiences at much less cost and greater scope. Thus, once more, we return to that which Nix attempted to avoid: the centrality of the computer in promoting novel learning experiences for students. And, as the model proffered by Franz and Papert (1988) which we described earlier in this chapter trivialized the computer's role, Nix's learning model restricts the computer to a studio-type production setting and, thus, likewise fails to viably integrate the computer (economically or pedagogically) as a flexible learning medium applicable to the everyday heterogeneous classroom learning contexts of students and teachers within the general U.S. school populace. Both models fail in that they assume that integration, cooperation, and communication will occur as a result of the computer-enhanced settings they propose. This assumption, as we have seen in detail, has proved to be erroneous in the case of interracial and interethnic groupings, as well as in language diverse groupings.

In summary, neither physical structures nor electronically controlled material objects within the learning setting will lead to student and teacher behaviors necessary for all students to enhance the probability of their socioacademic success. For this to occur, conscious, structured intervention strategies based on concrete principles of social learning must be implemented. Cooperative learning principles, as we have seen, provide theoretical support for socioacademic achievement within heterogeneous learning settings. At the implementation level, however, numerous factors, including but not limited to status differentials, have produced barriers to effective cooperative learning among peers in these settings. Recently, researchers and educators have begun to address cooperative learning principles, and, more generally, social interaction among peers, within computer-integrated classrooms. It is to these current instructional perspectives that we now turn.

Schwartz' "Intellectual Mirrors" Model

Description. Mathematics has traditionally been a difficult subject area for teachers to teach and for students to learn (cf. Papert, 1980, Chapter 2). Schwartz (1989) believes that effective learning of mathematics is linked to creative activities involving problem posing and problem solving. According to Schwartz, computer software has potential advantages over traditional paper and pencil-dependent forms of learning math creatively when it adheres to particular subject matter and pedagogical criteria. Two requirements seem especially important. First, the mathematical software must know about the particular domain under study and allow elements within the domain to be manipulated by the user. Second, the software design must not be artificially interactive, that is, presupposing knowledge of a user's intentions, progress, need to know, or accuracy, as is generally the case with commercially available drill and practice and simulation software programs. Schwartz codeveloped (with Michal Yerushalmy) a series of software programs collectively entitled The Geometric Supposer, which illustrate how software can enhance mathematical learning through student-driven exploration and problem-solving activities. Essentially, in the example Schwartz gives the reader, the creative process within which the "average ability" students engaged entailed following the teacher's instructions to subdivide and label each line making up a square (A,B,C,D) into three equal segments (E,F,G,H,I,J,K,L) and to then create what is definitely a quadrilateral and which may also be a second square within the original square by drawing lines attaching particular segments (EG, GI, IK, KA). The students then addressed the following teacher-posed question: "What interesting things can be said about the quadrilateral EGIK?" (p. 54).

Schwartz contends that the difference between this learning approach and traditional learning approaches with respect to geometry is that the onus of determining what is "interesting and true" about a mathematical result (in this case, a quadrilateral within a quadrilateral) rests with the students. Through the software program, the students can measure the respective angles of both quadrilaterals to determine if they are both squares. The software also allows students to draw other quadrilaterals, measure their angles, and then compare the results to quadrilateral EGIK. Nevertheless, these repeated drawings and measurements are insufficient, according to Schwartz, in that: "The students feel that a formal proof is needed, and they produce one, using pencil and paper, without too much difficulty" (p. 54).

There are more examples of this particular "creative" learning process that Schwartz offers the reader, all surprisingly reminiscent in tone and context of Franz and Papert's (1988) article reviewed earlier in this chapter in that the role of teacher and peer involvement in the learning process are apparent throughout the activities. Schwartz differs, however, from Franz and Papert in that creative learning subsumes a structural change in teacher and student roles: As neither teacher nor textbook (nor, perhaps Schwartz should add, software) is by virtue of its position an absolute authority, teachers and students engage in the learning process together to explore the course of their collective and individual problem posing and problem-solving mathematical activities. The role of social interaction is clear in Schwartz' learning model: "I believe that, for most of us, problem posing and problem solving are in large measure social activities. We need the stimulation of our peers, our students, and our teachers" (p. 58).

Critique of the Schwartz model. Schwartz' model relies primarily on the social aspects of learning where the value of computer software lies in the relative degree of its subject-matter depth and the corresponding degree to which that knowledge is accessible to and manipulatable by the students. The computer and its software within this learning model certainly lend speed and, perhaps, accuracy to the learning context described by Schwartz. The question remains, however, as to what salient learning features are offered or optimized through this computer-integrated learning model that are not achieved in noncomputer-integrated learning settings, other than the two well-established ones of velocity and precision with respect to calculations and graphics. The response, we feel, is none.

The essence of Schwartz' model is its reliance upon the social aspects of teaching and learning, especially in its plea for a collective learning setting characterized by exploration and discovery. These aspects are noted but not developed; yet, and in this we agree with Schwartz, these social aspects are absolutely essential to the learning process and its outcomes regardless of the subject matter. Although Schwartz acknowledges the crucial role of social interaction, its role is neither developed nor prominent in this model. Rather, centrality is once again given to the tool rather than the manipulators of the tool; and, once again, the assumption is that the tool will engender problem-fee, harmonious, and democratic social interaction among peers. Yet, from the evidence we have presented in earlier chapters, this assumption remains invalid, especially within heterogeneous learning contexts. The alternate assumption presented by Schwartz, embedded within the greater invalid assumption and thereby accorded secondary status, is that social interaction of a cooperative character is what is necessary for general socioacademic achievement.

Weir's "Computer as Humanizer" Model

Description. Weir's (1989) perspective of how computers equipped
with a particular type of software program (Logo) can transform
learning and learners perhaps represents the extreme end of the
continuum peopled by computer-integrated learning advocates. Weir's
perspective initially appears both appealing and practical in that the
computer's role and status in learning is couched within a Vygotskian
social learning framework. Appealing in that learning remains highly
dependent upon people interacting with people. The role of teachers
within the learning enterprise, for example, remains, at first blush,
intact: "That does not mean, however, that computers will replace
teachers...Learning cannot be separated from the social interactions
in which the individual is engaged" (p. 62). Also appealing, from a
student's perspective, is that computer-integrated learning can provide: "rich ways to match the learning situation to a student's
preferred working mode, and (so to speak) to the strengths of individual learners" (p. 64).

Finally, from a Vygotskian perspective, the use of "more capable" peers to help classmates offers a seemingly practical method
that distributes instruction more efficiently and equitably within the
average-size classroom. When the latter approach is complemented
by computer-mediated learning, Weir suggests that the students gain
in other ways as well:

> The ready access leads children to acquire from each other,
> considerable information about how to produce a range of effects
> on the computer...So now, in addition to internalizing social
> knowledge from the adults around them, students suddenly find
> themselves the producers of knowledge that their teachers and
> parents do not yet have. This ownership is sweet indeed. (p. 62)

Critique of the Weir model. Upon deeper analysis, however, there
are various pitfalls in Weir's perspective, not the least of which are, as
we shall see, a rather liberal interpretation of the Vygotskian notion
of social interaction and an unfortunate infatuation with Logo. Weir
posits that computers enable teachers to concentrate more easily on
their students' learning process rather than merely on the results of
that process, supporting this contention, in part, by alluding to the
socially affective consequences of a learner's problem-solving steps
being visible to others on the computer screen:

There is something about the public nature of the activity. There it is, up on the screen for all to see, each problem-solving step available for scrutiny in a way that pencil work scribbled in a corner of the page never is. This has earned the computer a label: it can act as a window into the mind. (p. 63)

We find Weir's contention to be facile. First, children monitor and edit (i.e., alter) their individual problem-solving activities at two points during the learning process: before receiving feedback from the computer and upon receiving "real-time" feedback (e.g., in the form of a graphic). It would be virtually impossible for a teacher to monitor the learning processes of thirty students individually working at their computers under these conditions. Second, in the event that the students were grouped in pairs, the teacher's ability to decipher individual learning processes would increase in complexity since "ownership" of those images ultimately presented on the screen would be extremely difficult to ascertain. In neither instance would the computer universally serve to more clearly reflect the mind's workings than would be the case with pencil-dependent methods.

Weir also anthropomorphizes computers into communicative participants in the children's learning process, asserting that the interaction between computers and children are conversationlike, and, as such, responsible for the computer-child classroom setting being filled with problem-solving talk. Her assertion, and her logic, are faulty on at least two counts. As we have previously summarized in chapter 1, a conversation between people tends to be a two-way event, characterized by the reciprocal capability of each participant to exchange interpretable messages, provide feedback, verbally seek, open and close channels of communication, indicate that a message has ended and that the partner may proceed to speak, and interrupt a message in progress, whether one's own or the other speaker's. Since classroom interaction between students and their teacher failed to meet the above two-way criteria, we described classroom language as communicative semblance, where students were essentially passive recipients of teacher-controlled talk.

How do commercially available computers of the type generally found in elementary and secondary schools reflect the above interactive requirements? Ostensibly, regardless of the type of software used (e.g., drill & practice, simulation, tutorial, etc.), they meet the criteria. But not so much in a human sense as a mechanical sense, and mainly in a one-way rather than in a reciprocal relationship. For instance, operating systems and educational software programs are written so that they can be interrupted, either by the instructional software command or at the operating system level. In many cases, however, this requires the student to pass through (although not necessarily complete) each of the previous learning sequences and an additional investment in unproductive time while the program reaches the desired location. Users can of course seek, start, and end communications with programs; but programs cannot seek, initiate or choose to close communication channels with users. The types of programs which we are discussing have no real flexibility, being limited to their internally designed structure. Thus, at both the one-way and reciprocal levels, there can be no communicative branching, so to speak, where either participant changes topic or style as a means to energize a conversation, modify its course or pace, or abandon it.

Software program flexibility is mechanical and predictable, and, while domain-specific, only domain-encompassing and domain-accessible to a very limited degree (Nix, 1988). To this extent, program development is more akin to the communicative semblance found in today's teacher-centered classrooms where knowledge is predictable, feedback is cursory, and answers are short and must conform to that which is already known by the teacher. With this type of software (and this is the norm), as with this type of teacher-student instructional practice, the desired learning processes and outcomes involving creativity, discovery, thought, and intellectual development on the part of the student are not assisted by natural conversational contexts and may well be hampered by the communicative artificiality characterizing these instructional approaches.

While the role of talk is actively encouraged in Weir's learning model, the identification of the speakers (human-human, human-machine), the dynamics of verbal interaction (who addresses whom, relative percentage and type of talk by speaker), and other aspects regarding the qualitative nature of that talk are not addressed. How talk is generated is also problematic within Weir's model. Her suggestion that individual students can engage in conversation with computers is not, as we have seen, tenable in an instructionally constructive, reciprocal sense. Thus, this leaves the students either talking out loud to themselves, to their teacher, or to their peers.

Within learning contexts, we have seen that student talk in general is not prized and that intergroup talk is scant. Who speaks with whom is dependent, in part, on variables associated with status, such as cultural, racial, ethnic, language, gender, perceived intelligence, and others. When Weir applies her computer-integrated instructional model to heterogeneous contexts, and especially with regard to those "whose academic experience has been unfavorable, or whose cultural status alienates them from the schooling enterprise altogether" (p. 65), she sees the teacher as a facilitator, as someone whose: "task is not so much to discover the student's goal as to contrive circumstances in which the child can begin to entertain any academic goal at all and see it as relevant" (p. 65).

Thus, Weir's model appears to place academically at-risk students in a one-to-one relationship with the computer, where they can: "mess around and 'play' in appropriately structured computer-based environments [and] develop their own goals and have experience in choosing and working to realize them" (p. 65).

The computer, then, is seen as having the ability to motivate, guide, and ultimately empower the student to take charge of his or her academic performance. This computer-as-bootstrap scenario is philosophically distant from Vygotsky's social-learning model, and not sustained by research evidence investigating student outcomes within computer-integrated learning settings. Attempting to incorporate the Vygotskian principle of learning through a more capable peer, Weir goes on to suggest that group projects will enable students to interact with and assist each other. Within a homogeneous learning context, this assumption could certainly, but not necessarily, occur. Given the evidence which we have presented regarding heterogeneous learning contexts in earlier chapters, however, it is unlikely that peers would talk to or help each other across racial, ethnic, linguistic, or socioeconomic divisions without a conscious instructional intervention strategy built on the fundamental elements of integration, cooperation and communication. The model which Weir presents, and implicitly advocates by way of example, however, is driven by physical design rather than by instructional purpose, i.e., a central computer work area through which all students in a project must pass when moving from one point to another. Social and verbal interaction among peers, under this condition, is mainly due to happenstance. The key element in the model Weir presents is unpredictability:

> The second feature of the setup is the level of engagement and focused interaction that goes on in that space. Children learn from each other how to do things that excite them. The claim is not that this happens all the time, but that on good days, the large open space becomes a kind of cultural cauldron, where the kind of informal cultural interchange that happens in a community occurs in a school setting. (p. 66)

Unpredictability can be a positive element in the learning process, especially when associated with natural communication and discovery learning. Here, however, Weir has managed to stand the notion on its head. Educators must implement *by design* activities that value integration, communication and cooperation among all members of the classroom on a regular basis throughout their curricular and extracurricular experiences. The notion of *predictability*, then, must precede that of unpredictability if an instructional model valuing socioacademic achievement and its key elements is to work to the benefit of all classroom members.

The notion of unpredictability, as applied to instructional settings by Weir, is akin in type and degree to the *laissez-faire* instructional model we addressed earlier (see chapter 1). The *laissez-faire* model has been practiced by teachers in bilingual programs (e.g., Milk, 1980) and, more directly, in linguistically heterogeneous, small group, project-oriented learning settings such as Finding Out/Descubrimiento (e.g., Neves, 1984). Both the unpredictability model and the *laissez-faire* model suggest that, given a physical context and instructional program, students from heterogeneous backgrounds, especially along linguistically and socioeconomically diverse lines, will naturally gravitate toward each other to engage in academically relevant learning experiences that are mutually beneficial. This notion has been correctly criticized for its conceptual weakness and empirical unsustainability at least since Allport (1954), and there is no present evidence that would warrant a theoretical or practical shift toward its instructional perspective.

There are other factors that suggest the inapplicability of the notion of unpredictability within current heterogeneous instructional settings. In chapters 2 and 3, for example, we have illustrated how factors such as negative attitudes and stereotypes can serve to reinforce perceived differences when students from diverse backgrounds are grouped within the same physical instructional setting. We have also seen how resegregation is promoted and supported by the educational institution itself through separatist devices such as tracking and ability grouping, especially in the language and math areas.

Thus, the preponderant evidence with respect to models of integration within racial and ethnolinguistically heterogeneous learning environments since 1954 has neither historically nor currently advocated the notion of unpredictability. To the contrary, for communication and cooperation to be achieved within heterogeneous classroom contexts, social interactions among heterogeneous peers must be formally encouraged, structured, monitored, and evaluated by the teacher, as well as understood, experienced, and internalized as a natural part of the learning process by the students themselves. This set of practices reflects a *conscious* pedagogical model that (1) understands how social interactions among heterogeneous student groups within the classroom reflect social interactions in the community, and (2) works to change the in-class social interactions among heterogeneous students groups from avoidance- and conflict-based to integrated, communicative and cooperative.

We contend that predictable learning environments of this type will lead to a broader base of active engagement in the learning process by students, regardless of their backgrounds, or perceived or tested ability levels in a particular language or subject matter. Likewise, these learning environments will also result in broader and heightened socioacademic achievement performance for the students participating in them.

In summary, the model of instructional/learning predictability which we advocate enables quality learning experiences to occur at the heterogeneous classroom level *as the rule not the exception*. It also enables the unpredictable to be subsumed, shared, explored, appreciated, absorbed and channeled by the learning group, who can then incorporate these exceptional experiences into their highly qualitative academic and social everyday learning experiences. Integration, cooperation and communication by design, not by happenstance, is the key to positive socioacademic experiences and achievement at the collective classroom level.

Computer-mediated peer learning is viewed by Weir as especially advantageous as it serves as a midpoint between the "culture of the street and that of the classroom, [which] particularly engages students who do not usually identify with academic goals" (p. 68). Furthermore, according to Weir, it helps students bridge the gap between learning informally by doing and being formally conscious of the logical principles associated with their learning. This is to be accomplished through the use of graphic objects and procedures, which are, Weir assumes, easily interpretable cultural symbols that all students can learn, manipulate, and transmit to one another in ways that Logo-deprived schools cannot:

The big trouble in schools is that formal activity is introduced in a way that makes it feel like an alien enterprise for many students, and the more formal, the less accessible it becomes. In contrast, Logo provides a setting for formal activity that does not have this effect. (p. 68)

Weir believes that the role of the teacher within the above setting is to delicately build (i.e., without usurping the student's own knowledge-acquiring methods) upon the knowledge that the student brings to class and to assist students in improving their capacity to self-reflect in order that they make a transition from informal learning to formal learning. The teacher can best do this, according to Weir, by learning how to program, especially in Logo, which "can act as a model for teachers' thinking about their instructional strategies" (p. 69). The turtle is the tool that supposedly can be manipulated on the screen by the student to create external expressions of his or her own otherwise difficult-to-express thought processes, much like dolls are used in child psychotherapy to verbalize repressed or other wise difficult-to-express thoughts and experiences. The teachers, on the other hand, receive assistance in their pedagogical development from other teachers by way of telecommunications. This would be necessary as Weir believes that inquiry-based, computer-mediated instruction complemented by cooperative learning is an instructional option which only a few teachers would select.

Thus, Weir's proposal is for particular teachers working within a particular instructional medium (computers) in much the same way that tracking and ability grouping targets students for specific curriculum paths. This strategy, whether for teachers or students, is the antithesis of the aims supported by democratic education in that it contributes, as we have seen, to segregation rather than integration, enhances competition rather than cooperation, and erects and sustains communicative barriers rather than building communicative links. The guidelines for integration, cooperation and communication at the school site level initially provided by Allport (1954), which are still necessary today, and which are unrepresented in Weir's exclusionary instructional model, correctly stipulate that instructional reform embrace those at the student and teacher levels, as well as at the institutional level, and that all must contribute to that reform. A philosophy of computer-integrated education must foster and complement democratic educational development, not, however unwittingly, reinforce elitist instructional or learning paths.

6

Computer-Integrated Instruction
in Culturally Heterogeneous Classrooms

Remedial Programs and Limited English Proficient Students

The Office of Technology (OTA) study. The OTA (1987) study points out that over the past decade more than a hundred million dollars have been allocated by the federal government through Chapter 1 compensatory educational programs for computer-integrated instruction. Chapter 1 funds are designated to assist low-income, predominantly minority, students improve their academic achievement. These computer-integrated instructional assistance programs have mirrored an educational assumption, and a corresponding instructional methodology, prevailing within compensatory eduction program of precomputer-integrated days: The acquisition of standard English and academic basic skills are the *sine qua non* for short and long-term academic success, and those students who are designated as deficient in either or both of these elements will acquire mastery through repeated drill and practice.

There are a host of historically controversial assumptions associated with why particular groups of children are targeted for compensatory education, stemming especially from the perceived lack of parental involvement with their children in appropriate school-readiness experiences. Thus, low-income children, especially those from homes where a language other than English is exclusively or also spoken, or where the family's culture is different from the school's, or whose race or ethnicity labels them as nonwhite, are at a perceived learning disadvantage upon entering school in comparison to their white, middle-class and above, dominant-language and dominant-culture peers. The logical irony of this educational perspective is that low-income children, the growing number of whom are also a designated language minority, are already in need of catching up to their advantaged peers at the outset of their formal education.

Compensatory education, whether through computer-integrated or other types of instructional media, has fared poorly in terms of achieving its catch-up goal. As a matter of fact, as we pointed out in an earlier chapter, those children designated as disadvantaged fall further behind in school the longer they stay in (Levin, 1985). Studies that attribute academic gains to participants in special education programs such as Chapter 1 are generally within—social class comparisons between control and experimental groups, and not a measure of how the experimental group is catching up to the advantaged sector. Levin (1989) recently calculated that the gap between advantaged and disadvantaged students, if it were to proceed at its current rate, would take well into the next century to close. School curricula based primarily on the notion of remediation, then, are not likely to translate into classroom experiences for low-income children that enable them to derive the same type and degree of educational outcomes experienced by their higher income counterparts.

The issue of computer equity for Chapter 1 and Limited English Proficient students is only partially addressed in the OTA study. Prior research literature (e.g., DeVillar, 1986; DeVillar and Faltis, 1987) has addressed computer equity from the standpoint of the key elements contained within it: access, participation and benefit. The OTA study fails to address equity, choosing instead to focus on access, which it simplistically defines, for all practical purposes, in terms of hardware units available within a school. While passing acknowledgement is given, albeit in embedded passages within the study, to more relevant issues within access, participation and benefit, and to related issues of software and teacher training, the OTA analysis ultimately reflects a *status quo* position rather than a critical perspective. Thus, the use of computers for remediation purposes is judged as "clearly...appropriate" (p. 7) and:

> "two decades of research on computer-assisted instruction (CAI) show that students make learning gains, as measured by test scores, when they use programs that are primarily drill and practice. The particular benefits of CAI for disadvantaged youngsters have been well documented in the research literature" (p. 8).

This, we offer, is a highly short-term and narrow perspective of what educational benefits are. Researchers investigating computer-integrated classroom settings are increasingly aware that the presence of computers can promote and even augment inequities among students (e.g., DeVillar, 1986; DeVillar and Faltis, 1987; LCHC, 1989). The research further indicates that income designation, gender, race, ethnicity and language are factors that often preclude language-minority and other minority students from deriving the type and extent of access, participation and benefit enjoyed by their middle class, Anglo-American, English-language proficient counterparts.

We have previously mentioned that the OTA study (1987) associated access with number of computer units available, and that the computer access differences between poorer and wealthier schools are rapidly disappearing. Access, however, cannot be reduced to the comparable numbers of computers. Computer environments within poorer schools, for example, have been documented as having not only fewer computers, but also computers that are older and more likely to malfunction. Other conditions typical of poorer schools that differentiate them from their wealthier counterparts include having less software, fewer qualified instructors, fewer computer-related textbooks, and fewer funds with which to repair machines and hire qualified instructors or train existing ones (DeVillar, 1986).

Until benefits translate into comparable grade-level achievement, proportionately equal numbers of high school and higher education graduates, and similar scores on standardized tests in all subject areas, the educational experience for this group of students must be recognized as fraught with problems that cannot be dismissed or explained away by a discrete, within-group test score. While computer-integrated learning of a drill and practice nature may have a place within the overall learning experience of students, it must be secondary to discovery-oriented learning. In the same way, the individualized, decontextualized learning activities which typically characterize the drill and practice computer-integrated programs must be secondary to cooperatively-based, contextualized learning experiences. In neither case, should a particular group of students be relegated to drill and practice as the primary type of instruction on the basis of their poverty level or other social (e.g., language, race, ethnicity) or academic (e.g., test scores) indicators.

Other attributes associated with computer-integrated learning mentioned in the OTA study include (a) higher student motivation, (b) the nonjudgmental character of the computer, (c) its ability to provide immediate feedback, (d) the ability of each student to work at his or her own pace, and (e) the indirect outcome of the student experiencing an increased status due to his or her involvement with, and manipulation of, the computer. While the study's authors acknowledge that the presence of these attributes form part of a belief system (as opposed to a knowledge base) shared generally by researchers and practioners, they do not analyze the extent to which this belief system is supported by empirical or even anecdotal evidence. These attributes of course are inexorably bound one to the other and must be investigated rather than naively presumed to hold true.

The problems and limitations of educational software. It has been our experience that the design limitations of educational software can generate inordinate and unproductive confusion in students, to the extent that computer interactions can negatively influence their pace and motivation, as well as their achievement and social status. For example, at one particular visit to a school using a schoolwide, elaborate drill and practice, computer-integrated instructional program, the software program could not distinguish between or intelligently react to words that were inadvertently separated (e.g., "sun flower" vs. "sunflower"). Thus, the student could provide the correct answer but have it negated due to the separation of the two words comprising a compound word. The teacher or his or her aide are in no better position to see and assist in this situation than they would be in a noncomputer-integrated classroom. In fact, given the presence of thirty screens and a nonteacher-focused instructional setting, monitoring students' activities is more demanding. In this, and many other computer settings, as in many noncomputer instructional settings, the students are left to sit, mostly with one hand raised, until their silent request for assistance is acknowledged and help arrives.

In the above example, the educational program failed to distinguish between content and form, between what the student actually knew and how he or she presented it. In this particular case, the system's simplistic right or wrong approach to learning was not responding to the student's educational need in a relevant way, and served more to hinder his or her pace, motivation and self-image than to enhance them. The message is clear: Not only must teachers maintain responsibility for analyzing the pedagogical soundness of software prior to and during its use by students, but they must also remain diligently engaged, physically and pedagogically, in the students' learning process as they interact with the computer.

The computer, at its present state of program development generally available to elementary and secondary schools, is no more capable of significantly motivating the student, nor of providing any of the previously mentioned attributes, than a physically integrated setting is capable of ensuring social integration within the classroom. The key to immediate and long-term socioacademic development resides in the interdependent relationship which results from the interplay of the following factors: (1) the academic and cultural preparation and skills of the instructor, (2) the qualitative and quantitative appropriateness of the instruction, including the degree and type of instructional grouping strategies and instructional materials, (3) the degree of cross-discipline and cross-grade curricular continuity, (4) the degree to which the school site and district administrators' curricular aims and activities reflect those of the classroom teacher, and (5) the degree to which the students, parents, other members of the community, and institutions within the private and public sector, understand and support these curricular aims and activities.

Pedagogical limitations of computer-integrated remedial instruction. Drill and practice programs address instruction only as an individualized event in which the student responds in a reactive mode to the computer's queries based upon a certain programmed store of facts and interpretations. The computer's role is both as supplier of facts to be learned and as judge of how well they have been learned. The student has essentially no control over the computer nor engages in any meaningful (i.e., creatively manipulative) interaction with it. This orientation is as inherently inflexible as it is unexciting, and reflects the philosophical tradition that knowledge is the accumulation of facts and interpretations, that learning is comprised of right and wrong answers, and, most lamentably, that education is a rote, rather than a discovery, process.

As important, yet perhaps less directly evident, the drill-and-practice orientation, irrespective of its technological or manual manifestations, also reflects a singular perspective toward children and the family, community and culture from which they come. The assumption that children enter school with deficiencies, based on cultural, language, and other normative expectations, which must be overcome if they are to be academically successful is parochial. Our schools are comprised in ever greater numbers by children who come from low-income households where English is not necessarily the primary language. Thus, the language, culture, and income of school-age and preschool-age children reflect the actual and growing physical, cultural and economic heterogeneity of our populace.

Instructional approaches that visualize these differences as deficiencies to be eradicated and that attempt to mold these complex human beings into the likeness of a middle-class, native-English-speaking ideal are doomed to continued failure. Within these alternate settings, language, cultural, and socioeconomic elements have

helped form, through complex sociopsychological processes and experiences, a major part of each child's personal and social identity and
expectations. To assume that this identity can be displaced or significantly altered in favor of one that is considered more appropriate by
the school before grade-level learning can begin is faulty and detrimental on numerous counts. The gravest pedagogical error, however,
is that this approach does not capitalize upon what the children do
bring to school with them.

   Pedagogical alternatives to computer-integrated remediation.
Psychologically, socioculturally and academically, some groups of
children are singled out at the outset of their schooling experience as
different from the school populace norm, when in fact that norm is not
only rapidly changing, but, in California and several other states (e.g.,
Arizona, Nevada, New Mexico), has already changed. If the massive
retention and failure rates among these groups at present, and the
vast human and national resource waste which school failure produces, are to be effectively countered, the school system must now
adapt its instructional practice to the racial, cultural, language and
socioeconomic heterogeneity which characterizes the United States
rather than continue its educational attempts to mold all students in
the reflection of an imagined *status quo.*

   This is not to say or advocate that English take a subsidiary role
or that educational standards be lowered. It is to say and advocate
that instructional approaches incorporating the key elements of
integration, communication and cooperation be offered that take
advantage of and celebrate our heterogeneity. Educational practice
must ensure that all students are accorded equal status relative to
their educability, especially at school entry, regardless of their income
status, race, ethnicity, culture or home language. Moreover, teachers,
staff and administrators, as professionals, must model what they
advocate to their students: they must become actively and creatively
involved in learning as a lifelong process. As professionals, however,
their learning must not solely concentrate upon a particular discipline
or grade level, but must incorporate knowledge addressing how to best
foster knowledge generation among students within the heterogeneous classroom setting.

   Within this paradigm, neither the use of standard English nor
the supposed school-readiness norms of the Anglo-American middle
class will be viewed as the reference level which all others must attain
prior to becoming educable. Likewise, neither variable can be used as
the rationale for retaining or failing students, or for their leaving
school prior to course completion.

The perception of students by educators, then, must be sharply refocused to view heterogeneity in income, language, culture, ethnicity, and race as the norm. The problem of educators remains the same: how to effectively educate students. The means and ends, however, are different: school teachers, staff, and administrators must focus upon instructional methods that (a) promote integration, communication and cooperation among all students and (b) capitalize upon the knowledge base and context that the different children bring to school with them as a means to promote learning.

Thus, within this alternative paradigm, there is no *a priori* need for remediation based on the view that social heterogeneity of the type we have described is detrimental to our national interest, or economically or instructionally infeasible to accommodate, or a socio-psychocultural deficiency that presents a lasting barrier to learning until removed. To the contrary, each child is accepted, as is each group, and targeted for socioacademic success via guided, discovery-oriented curricula that are heterogeneously sensitive. These curricula would regularly integrate students in cooperatively-based, small groups for communicative purposes. Under these conditions, then, the school will have democratized its socialization practices by adapting itself instructionally to value and mine the actual and potential intellectual richness of all its students.

The salient role of language in computer-integrated instruction. Communication in the classroom is logically and theoretically more a language-based event than any other type of nonverbal event. As we have discussed in earlier chapters, however, talk by students is overshadowed by teachers talking and by communicative semblance. Thus, opportunities in the classroom for meaningful verbal production between student peers and between students and their teacher are slight. The presence of computers in the classroom or school laboratory, however, has reportedly served as a catalyst to verbal production between students. The national survey of computer use under the direction of Becker (1985), for example, reported that talk occurred between students in computer-integrated classroom settings in the majority of instances regardless of the individualized or group nature of the instructional activity. Becker's survey findings with respect to spontaneous and encouraged verbal activity within computer-integrated settings have been corroborated by numerous other investigators (e.g., Johnson, Johnson, and Stanne, 1986; Alvarez and Vasquez, 1990; Riel, 1985).

This finding must nevertheless be interpreted with reasonable caution. We have repeatedly seen in earlier chapters that this principle does not apply within either traditional or alternative (e.g., bilingual, Finding Out/*Descubrimiento*) instructional settings where students are not homogeneous, especially with regard to language or language proficiency. Similarly, the OTA study found that computer use in remedial English as a second language classes (i.e., Chapter 1) and regular classroom settings where limited-English proficient (LEP) speakers were enrolled was lower than for any other classification of Chapter 1 teacher. Thus, while the lowest figure for computer-using teachers in Chapter 1 or regular classrooms is 50 percent, where ESL and LEP students are concerned, the percentage drops to 40 percent among teachers who teach ESL in conjunction with other courses, 24 percent with teachers who only teach ESL, and 22 percent for teachers who teach LEP students.

Opportunities, then, within remedial classroom settings for computer use and for the concomitant peer-related language development experiences within these same settings are scant, as less than 25 percent of the total ESL-specific and LEP-specific teachers surveyed used computers in their classrooms. The point of course is that non-English proficient students in remedial and regular classrooms are not participating to a significant degree in computer-related activities and comparatively much less than their English-speaking proficient peers. Thus, English language proficiency has become an obvious criterion for computer-integrated activities.

As the OTA study suggests, barriers to computer use are not solely linguistic but also compounded by socioeconomic status, racial and ethnic factors. Ultimately, then, the poorer, non-Anglo-American, limited-English proficient students have least access to computer use in the schools. Computer-integrated remediation programs do not and cannot offer a viable path toward comparable educational development for these and other Chapter 1 profile students with respect to their middle-class peers. The viability of Chapter 1 as a large scale, long-term pedagogical practice, sanctioned by national policy, must be scrutinized in light of sounder pedagogical alternatives.

Alternative, discovery-based, instructional methods can enrich students' education by building upon those sociocultural, cognitive and linguistic structures with which they arrive at school, and through complex grouping strategies which include guided, cooperative-peer interactions. Innovation, not remediation, is what Chapter 1 profile students need. Johnson (1985) cited an exceptional project in type and results within the Chapter 1 setting which appears to embrace the value of innovation, the Higher Order Thinking Skills (HOTS) project under the direction of Stanley Pogrow. Based on the

OTA study, however, the HOTS project appears to have limited extension (i.e., thirty-three Chapter 1 sites) and has thus maintained its status as an exception to the Chapter 1 drill and practice rule.

Enrichment-Based Computer-Integrated Instruction and Limited English Proficient Students

The roles of verbal interaction and cooperative learning behaviors among peers are increasingly being incorporated into research paradigms that investigate computer-integrated and intergroup-learning settings. Riel (1985), for example, reports on preliminary findings with respect to the Computer Chronicles Newswire (CCN) project. This project, incorporating sociopsychological and contextual-learning notions associated with Dewey, Piaget and Vygotsky, established a telecommunications linkage between third and fourth grade students in three rural schools, one urban school, and one suburban school in Alaska and California, as a means to improve their writing skills as they learned about their own and others' culture and surroundings. The students participating in this study had previously been classified by the regular classroom teachers as experiencing learning difficulties in reading and writing.

The design of the project embodied a two-fold mandate: (1) that pairs of students from the same school work together in order to write and edit stories regarding their locale, which they could then share locally and across the newswire, and (2) that students serve, voluntarily, on an editorial review board to critique, select and edit articles submitted locally and by participants from other locales for publication in their newspaper. Undergraduate "adaptive experts" were enlisted to assist the students in engaging in and completing their writing assignments; their responsibilities shifted by design from direct involvement (e.g., helping students to write) to indirect support (e.g., encouraging students to use the dictionary) during the course of the study. Writing, then, was designed to be a concretely social activity, directly supported by adult interventions at the preliminary stages and, at the latter stages, a product of peer collaboration.

Pretest-posttest comparisons demonstrated formidable development on the part of learners in the areas of text length, activity-based writing and attitude toward writing. Riel emphasizes that findings are only preliminary and suggestive, especially in light of the absence of a control group, which would have enabled comparisons in each of the three areas mentioned above. Nevertheless, the average length of stories increased from fifty-three words to seventy-nine words, while that of activity-based description increased from an average of twenty-nine words to sixty-three words. Thus, students were not only writing more but writing more about the task at hand: describing an activity to an imagined new student. At the pretest level, students tended to produce more words which described the new student and wrote less about the actual activity. This process was reversed at the posttest level.

Also, at the pretest level, students voiced complaints with respect to becoming involved in writing activities, needed adult assistance to even become engaged in the writing task, and, in some cases, might not have even participated in the project had computers not been available to them. Their attitude toward writing had dramatically changed by the end of the project: pens were used without complaint, assignments were listened to and understood, and writing activities were immediately engaged in by the students.

Riel also reports that editing became a natural part of the writing process, as did producing a particular piece for a particular audience. Thus, while a written piece might be cause for celebration at the individual, home or even classroom level, it might require additional effort to be accepted at the editorial review board level. Students became accustomed to writing for different audiences and to receiving and accepting constructive criticism to tailor their articles to more aptly fit the needs of a particular audience.

The role of the classroom teacher did not appear to be integrated into the project design. Thus, teachers tended, we surmise, to see products rather than processes. Information regarding teacher conferencing, coordinated activities between the project and the regular classroom, and other integrative efforts are not mentioned by Riel. It is not too surprising, then, that when Riel reports upon a teacher's reaction to the development of two of her students who participated in the project, the teacher chose to voice her disappointment that one of the students had not demonstrated more improvement in his spelling, even though their attitude toward writing had improved, as had their facility in writing.

The CCN project was designed explicitly for students to work together in pairs in order to produce and edit stories at the computer. Riel reports that the cooperative nature of this design enabled the students to provide and receive the kind of help that was necessary but not readily available in the regular classroom where writing was essentially structured as an individual activity. We agree with this approach but are aware, through our own (e.g., DeVillar, 1987, 1988, 1989, 1990) and others' research (e.g., Edfelt, 1989, 1990; Merino, Legarreta, Coughran, and Hoskins, 1990), that cooperation is itself a learned behavior and that interactions between peers vary in type and outcomes based on various contextual factors and the individual skill level of each partner.

Students who are not proficient in English (i.e., non-English proficient, or NEP) but native speakers of Spanish, for example, may well produce less words orally at the computer than any more English-proficient partner he or she may have, irrespective of the language or partner involved (DeVillar, 1987). Thus, an NEP speaker may collaborate less in the development of a writing activity whether Spanish or English is the language of communication. Even when an NEP speaker may apparently be gaining practice in the second language through English-only dialogue with a monolingual English speaker (ME) speaker at the computer, other factors may override the apparent collaborative nature of the experience. Edfelt (1989) found, for example, that NEP speakers tended to feign comprehension and to employ other risk-avoidance behaviors when paired with an ME speaker at the computer in a cooperative activity.

The previous research which we have cited in earlier chapters (e.g., Fordham, 1988; Matute-Bianchi, 1986) with respect to intergroup and intragroup communicative barriers provides additional support for structured, guided approaches to cooperative work within heterogeneous classroom settings, whether or not the work is conducted at a computer. Thus, Riel's description of the dyads' behaviors within the CCN project as wholly cooperative appears to lack sufficient detail to warrant complete acceptance. Issues of language, keyboard, text and editorial dominance between dyad partners, for example, are likely to hinder cooperation and communication whenever untrained participants engage in collaborative work. How these issues are expressed, negotiated, and resolved are of strategic importance if educators are to understand and plan for effective and equitable dyadic and small-group cooperative learning experiences.

A number of recent projects have also utilized telecommunications to develop and improve writing skills of students at the elementary school level as they communicate across language groups, cultures and nations. In two cases, these long-distance computer-integrated activities have been reported as favorable to first and second language development. An article by the Laboratory of Comparative Human Cognition (LCHC) (1989), for example, cites evidence presented by Diaz (1988) and Riel (1986) that bilingual, Spanish-speaking students were eager to use Spanish, as well as English, in response to communications in Spanish from Spanish-speaking peers.

Certainly one of the more, if not the most, innovative and pedagogically complete computer-supported writing project involving students across distances is *Orilla a Orilla* (*From Shore to Shore*), or, as it is also referred to, *ORILLAS* (Cummins & Sayers, 1990; Sayers, 1988, 1989; Brown & Sayers, n.d.). Cummins (personal communication) reports that *ORILLAS* initially began as a computer-networking writing project modelled along the process-oriented, child-centered and collaboratively structured lines of similar projects developed by Riel (see above). Once introduced through an educator participating in *ORILLAS* to the pedagogy and praxis of the French educator Celestin Freinet (1896–1964), the project organizers adapted *ORIL-LAS* to the directly compatible and pedagogically more comprehensive Modern School Movement (MSM) model (Cummins, personal communication). This model, created by Freinet in 1924, continues as a cross-cultural network comprised of thousands of classrooms in thirty-three countries. Each classroom, including each teacher and every student, is paired in a relationship of regular (e.g., weekly, monthly) cooperative interscholastic exchange with another "Sister" classroom. On a less intense basis, each classroom also is communicatively linked to other classrooms within the same network. At regular intervals, individual students and the class as a whole exchange packages which include materials such as local realia, graphics/illustrations, and media (e.g., photographs, audiotape and videotape recordings), and written compositions.

ORILLAS and MSM are based upon three essentially and purposely identical learning principles: Students learn best (1) when working together in socially meaningful activities; (2) when the learning activities tie in to and build up their prior experiences; and, (3) when the learning activities encourage individual and group responses that will be shared with and responded to by diverse audiences, locally and across time, distance and circumstance (e.g., gender, socioeconomic status, culture, language, religion, age, etc.).

As meaningful communication is paramount in Freinetian pedagogy, it is important to clarify its relationship to communications technology: Regardless of how technology is manifested (e.g., chalk, pencil/pen, printing press, word processing, telecommunications), its use is restricted to that of a medium through which language is expressed and transmitted to others, principally in the form of written text. Computer-supported communications technology such as word processing and telecommunications provide students with a new source of motivation to compose, edit and publish written language. It is now possible, for example, for students to use sophisticated publishing-oriented software to store, edit, add graphics and print copies of drafts and final products in a manner that increasingly approaches conventional publishing house endeavors. Moreover, the incentive to use computers for communicating with others is furthered by the fact that students are writing for real audiences, and thus, have good reason to take on role and styles associated with organized journalism and creative writing, including executive editor, reporter, author, proofreader, and the like. Finally, computer-supported technology aimed at expanding communication opportunities may motivate students to produce more text than they could with conventional media because of the decreased time involved in generating a polished copy and the possibility of a wide reading audience.

These motivating factors, while noteworthy and important, remain subsidiary to the social learning principles embraced by the Freinetian pedagogy alluded to earlier. We infer from this pedagogy that the teacher's and students' motivation to participate in this scholastic exchange model is further and more importantly sustained through the following blend of activities and their potential educational benefits:

(1) the social and physical interaction of students within a shared context that is teacher-guided;
(2) the students' awareness that what they view within their environment, coupled with what and how they reflect and act upon it, individually and collectively, can effect its character;
(3) the development of personality through educational activities that value social discourse and cooperation as effective and efficient means to problem identification and resolution;
(4) the experience that one's own thought and expression of that thought can, on the one hand, influence, and, on the other hand, be improved upon by, the thought, expression, and action of others;
(5) the development of an active consciousness with respect to one's local and global context;
(6) the experience of gathering materials and information from one's own setting in a manner which addresses an issue of local and, perhaps, extended relevance;
(7) working successfully with one's peers and teachers in composing an articulated statement with respect to a particular and relevant topic;
(8) learning to generate units of information, individually or collaboratively, to share with peers and others, locally and across

distances, in styles that effectively communicate with the intended audience;

(9)   deriving value and sustenance from the response to one's communicative endeavors and from other information received from peers within and across corresponding classrooms; and,

(10) understanding that the above elements may be integrated throughout the school curriculum (e.g., language arts, science, math, social studies).

Within the Freinetian model, each classroom is locally self-sufficient in that discovery-oriented learning can occur through interaction with one's peers, community, and surrounding. This model of learning, however interesting, could breed parochialism among students and teachers if the component requiring scholastic exchange across communities were not present. The use of technology primarily enables students and teachers to extend their contact with other individuals and groups in different communities, surroundings and circumstances. Although computers are useful and potentially creative in this enterprise, exchanges are not dependent upon their use. Other, admittedly less rapid, means are available to transmit communications. Use of the mail, for example, is the major vehicle to send projects and cultural exchange packages which regularly accompany and supplement written communications.

   ORILLAS appears to extend the already significant democratic boundaries of MSM, the larger network to which it adheres philosophically and in practice. Its design and execution firmly reflect and address salient issues and circumstances with respect to the education of language minority students in U.S. society. *ORILLAS* aims to increase proficiency in their first and second languages, improve academic achievement, and enhance self-esteem (Cummins & Sayers, 1990; Faltis & DeVillar, 1990; Brown & Sayers, n.d.). Spanish-speaking language minority students in the United States participating in *ORILLAS*, for example, interact with peers in Spanish-speaking countries as a means to value and develop the former's use of Spanish through educationally relevant experiences associated with Freinetian pedagogy. The potential advantages to such communication are readily apparent. In those cases where Spanish is the dominant or preferred language of the student, for example, communicating about a personally relevant social topic could well result in language and cognitive benefits. Moreover, aspects of these language and cognitive benefits would transfer to and enhance the development of English and learning activities conducted in English. Similarly, a student's self-esteem could benefit from (1) having others within his or her school context value the use of Spanish, (2) successfully using it to generate information units for an intended audience, and (3) receiving responses in Spanish to the information sent by the student.

It is worthwhile to mention that the term "self-esteem" is problematic within education and mainstream society. To avoid the term becoming aligned with such negative constructs as "deficit theory," we must remember that self-esteem is inextricably linked to the societal view of and support for the students' collective circumstance. In the United States, for example, Spanish has been, and continues to be, associated with poverty, nonstandardness, self-imposed marginality, and a host of other negative stereotypes. Under these conditions, children and adolescents from Spanish-language backgrounds, however distant in time and space, are viewed as language transgressors and, as such, in need of language remediation.

When whole groups of children from particular cultural, ethnic and racial groups are designated as suffering from low self-esteem, we must consider the source of the malaise. We must not rule out the very real possibility that this is yet one more patently false image of children who do not fit the national mainstream image (i.e., white, Anglo-Saxon, Protestant, upper-middle class) or, if low self-esteem is present at the group level, that it reflects students' reactions to institutionalized intercultural conflict and domination. Most importantly, we cannot act from the unspoken assumption that low self-esteem is an affliction one is born with or to which one is genetically or culturally prone. It must be clear that any institutionally sanctioned activity that pays only lip-service to meaningful integration of a language other than English in a student's education will not have a significant effect on promoting high self-esteem, but will continue to foster educational inequities and their predictable consequences in the form of exceeding low academic achievement, abysmal school completion rates, and political and economic marginality.

The *ORILLAS* project, while not a panacea, does portend to offer a promising pedagogical means by which to obviate the traditional educational path and circumstance open to Spanish-speaking and other language minority students. Moreover, programs of this nature exemplify the type of discovery-oriented instructional context and communicative-cooperative climate that would benefit U.S. students in general. The extent to which *ORILLAS* and similarly modelled projects can be successful with heterogeneous student populations largely depends on (1) the quality and degree of teacher-training in social learning pedagogical principles, (2) the degree to which teachers adhere to and integrate social learning pedagogical principles into their classroom instructional repertoire, (3) the degree to which a quality curriculum is implemented across grade levels, (4) the program's duration, and (5) the support—financial, philosophic, political and otherwise—the projects receive from the school and school district management and staff.

The sheer cost to schools of a telecommunications-intense learning activity remains a great hindrance to its widespread integration within the classroom. These costs should decrease over time and even now are within reach of a small number of programs. *ORILLAS* classrooms, for example, pay from $200 to $300 each per year for their connect time; this enables a classroom to correspond with one other classroom (Sayers, personal communication). Communication within *ORILLAS* and related programs is primarily one-way in that information is prepared for transmission while not being connected to the communications network. Once the information is ready for transmission, the classroom connects to the network; this usually occurs during times when transmission costs are lowest. Periodic two-way communication between classrooms, even if pedagogically justifiable, is currently prohibitive economically.

There are, however, examples of collaborative ventures between private industry engaged in computer-integrated learning activity projects and public schools which served to offset expenses that would otherwise be beyond the budgetary limits of most public schools. These collaborations offer, on the one hand, physical and documentary (e.g., film, audio, verbal) access to students, teachers, staff, administrators, and even families, all of which enable equipment and software design inconsistencies to be worked out. The participating schools, in turn, can obtain the necessary hardware and software to actively engage students and teachers in the particular project. They may also receive training and documentation with respect to the equipment's use, and general access to industry specialists involved in the particular program. Both students and teachers tend to invest more hours (e.g., preparation time, assessing students' work) in these special projects, but appear to value participating in a project's process and the product it delivers, including the increased status and benefits that participation in such projects brings (e.g., sponsored conferences attendance, stipends, direct communication with private sector management, hosting distinguished visitors, cash and equipment awards, etc.). Both industry and schools, moreover, receive widespread media visibility, as magazines, newspapers, and even television, report on the nature of these innovative uses of computers within the schools.

The aforementioned article by the LCHC, for example, lists numerous projects in which private industry is collaborating with educators to promote telecommunications activities. AT&T, McGraw-Hill Information Exchange, and National Geographic Kids Network, for example, all offer ways in which teachers, and/or students can communicate with one another regarding educational topics via telecommunications (LCHC, 1989). *Common Ground* and Free Educational Mail Service (FrEdMail), on the other hand, have been developed by educators for use by teachers and, to a lesser degree, by students (LCHC, 1989).

The role of enrichment-based software within the heterogeneous classroom. The above enrichment-based telecommunications projects also point toward an area within computer-integrated instruction where educators can focus their expertise: programming educational software. Educators can become involved in programming either directly or by assisting pedagogically in its development. Educators need to become actively engaged in this effort regardless of their particular area within computer-integrated education (e.g., social sciences, physical or natural sciences, math instruction, etc.). Tom Snyder—a former teacher, author, and educational software designer/producer/entrepreneur—perhaps has been the most successful in incorporating a cooperative spirit and structure into the design of his software products. His educational software series *Decisions, Decisions*, for example, structures goal attainment around computer simulations that require students to engage in verbal and textual interactions as they pursue their group problem-solving activities. Simulations throughout the series of eight software programs encourage small-group participation. For example, a student may be responsible for enacting the role of a particular character and reading his or her comments to the other group members from prepared scripts provided by the software producer. There are of course variations to the above structure, and teachers and students can introduce their own modifications.

Snyder's format in this series satisfies the socioacademic condition that each person or group have verbal and topically relevant input into the final decision-making process. In the *Colonization* or *Immigration* simulation, for example, a student may belong to a group comprised of four other members, one of whom is, perhaps arbitrarily, designated as leader, with the other four functioning as advisors. The computer simulation, using graphics, screen text, and book text, then presents a situation which reflects a potentially politically volatile issue requiring a series of decisions. Each decision is evaluated and the program simulates public reaction. Before making a decision, however, the leader listens to the advice of his four advisors who have each read a prepared text and who then together assist the leader in coming to a decision. The prepared texts, moreover, present historical situations in United States or world history analogous to the polemic needing to be addressed. This particular design feature introduces students to historical contexts as a means to solving current issues, thereby reinforcing the value of understanding present events in light of past contexts.

The topics covered in the immigration and colonization packages are also relevant to the issues of heterogeneity experienced within the United States: race, ethnicity, class, and language. The students express their values regarding these topics through the process of completing either of the two simulations. One might predict, therefore, that the heterogeneity in the classroom could provide different perspectives within the same group with respect to the types of decisions made and the rationales associated with making them.

From a language development perspective, the value of this particular software lies greatly in its provision of prescripted monologues for students to read from, listen to, and react to. Talk is encouraged throughout the program, but is formally structured through these advisory monologues. The use of note-taking is also encouraged through screen texts in the form of reminders to students that they record particular game-related information.

Snyder's educational software programs are geared toward middle school and high school students (5–12) performing at grade level. The language level (particularly, vocabulary and syntax) is generally beyond the immediate proficiency grasp of most nonproficient and limited-proficient speakers of English. Concurrent translation of the textual material would inevitably prove an exhausting and trying exercise for even the more proficient bilinguals. The problem of translating extends beyond vocabulary and syntax considerations, as translating is a skill that is not necessarily positively correlated with bilingual proficiency. Input and output in the first and second languages of nonproficient and limited-proficient speakers of English, then, present a pedagogical conundrum with respect to effectively integrating these qualitative educational software programs into a heterogeneous, mixed English language proficiency, classroom.

The Snyder *Decisions, Decisions* series of software products intelligently and interestingly provide knowledge-generation activities in the social sciences through cooperatively based, flexibly structured simulations. The series' design is especially useful within high school classrooms where students' English-language proficiency, and reading and comprehension skills are designated as nativelike relative to their peers. There are, nevertheless, two areas where improvements might be considered. The first area concerns the ambiguity surrounding how the results are tallied (e.g., percentage of voters agreeing with decision sequence in *Immigration* simulation) and the manner in which final political outcomes are derived (e.g., the leader, and presumably his or her advisors, gaining or losing reelection). Although students expend time and intellectual energy in their attempts to make decisions based on various simulation-relevant criteria, the outcomes can, and do, reflect an arbitrariness that appears educationally self-defeating. That is, the students, rather than being rewarded for their efforts, may well be informed that outcomes can never really be predicted and that their team lost the election. Where students' control over outcomes has been eroded, their cooperative practice of thoughtful decision making through educationally oriented group dialogue may be discarded in favor of random or whimsical input. The second area concerns the possibility of promoting communicative artifice rather than natural communication through computer-supported simulations. As a communicative "ice-breaker" to enable all individuals within a group to verbally participate, scripted dialogues appear to function as a viable alternative. This quasi-communicative practice seems to gain increased credibility when the scripts reflect accurate summaries of historical events which relate to the current issue being discussed. Thus, students appear eloquent, sophisticated, and knowledgeable regarding political-historical events and issues, when in fact they do not have command of these three elements to any comparable degree. From a communicative and pedagogical perspective, moreover, one might well question the degree to which scripted monologues are helpful and recommended in computer-integrated classroom settings, especially where distinct varieties of English (e.g., standard, nonstandard) are exhibited among students or where some students are designated as less than nativelike in their English-language proficiency. There is of course no easy answer to such a question, depending as it does on empirical rather than conjectural evidence. The point which we have stressed throughout this work, however, is that communication which is genuine is more appropriate for intragroup and intergroup understanding, and that it more strongly supports the integrative and cooperative elements which promote collective socioacademic achievement. There is always room for acting, and for promoting unity and cooperation through drama. The thespian aspect of these Snyder-produced software programs, however, is rather distant from the central focus of understanding historical, political, and decision-making processes and their interrelationship. Students do not have to act to learn, but general socioacademic success does require that they learn to get along with one another (integrate), share the work load (cooperate) and talk sensibly to one another (communicate).

In summary, Snyder has, on the whole, carved out highly interesting and innovative territory in the area of computer-integrated instruction. His products in the middle and secondary school social science area which we discussed are commendable in their integrative, cooperative and communicative design and spirit, but appear to have limited application to heterogeneous audiences. We contend, moreover, that the use of scripted monologues of this type will not readily promote and develop these three elements among heterogeneously grouped middle or secondary school students unless complemented by naturally occurring dialogues and cooperatively structured activities, both appropriately guided and monitored.

Summary

In sponsored research projects, there is a definite trend toward actively engaging language-minority students within heterogeneous classroom settings in enrichment-based computer-integrated learning opportunities. These enrichment-based activities especially embrace the area of telecommunications, and, because the student networks extend beyond regional and even national borders, offer bilingual students opportunities to use and develop their first and second languages.

Communicative and integrative opportunities, however, are not yet strongly supported by structured cooperative methods, although working in pairs and small groups now appears to be a standard practice in computer-integrated learning activities. Seating arrangements and good intentions, as we have seen, are not sufficient to produce cooperative relationships between peers from heterogeneous backgrounds. There are definite research-supported indications (e.g., DeVillar, 1987, 1988, 1989, 1990; Edfelt, 1989, 1990), for example, that within linguistically heterogeneous computer-integrated learning contexts, the amount, type and quality of talk between peers in dyads will differ in accordance with particular factors. One of the more obvious of these is, of course, the respective English-language proficiency of the interlocutors. Other factors include (1) the type of software used, whether of a simulation or word-processing nature;

(2) the relative social status of the participants, which can, for example, result in unequal amounts of Spanish spoken among speakers who are equally proficient in Spanish but not in English; (3) the relationship of the students to the computer, which can be characterized as computer-centered (triadic), a condition not necessarily conducive at this juncture to language development, or as the more language-supportive human-centered; and, (4) the extent to which cooperative learning methods are formally integrated into the particular instructional/learning activity. Future research, then, must continue to investigate these and other factors which promote or inhibit first or second language communication between interlocutors within cooperatively structured classroom contexts.

There are also indications, albeit at the secondary school level, that software appears to be more socially directed than before, encouraging small group participation rather than individualized instruction. Cooperative learning techniques, however, also have a definite presence and value within elementary school computer-integrated settings, although due more to teacher/researcher-designed grouping strategies (e.g., Male, Johnson, Johnson, & Anderson, 1986) than to the internal design of the software. Although the presence of cooperatively driven software and activities is encouraging, there are, nevertheless, potential weaknesses that we have seen associated with each. Substantial research remains necessary to determine the extent to which even cooperatively driven software and activities are promoting integration, communication and cooperation within computer-integrated heterogeneous classrooms.

Conclusion

Current instructional practices are not generally conducive to establishing intergroup cooperation or communication. These practices present a common profile in that they stress (1) competitive learning contexts, (2) classroom organizations that physically separate learners from each other, and (3) teacher-centered instructional delivery systems that value a knowledge-dispensing philosophy rather than one which encourages discovery learning. Intergroup cooperation and communication are further thwarted by the within-class segregation of students according to perceived or evaluation-based skill-level differences. These conditions can negatively affect students' achievement and intergroup skills by constraining their socially-dependent learning experiences.

As we have consistently argued, collective learning within heterogeneous settings is a result of positive social interaction, that is communication and cooperation. These, in turn, are contingent upon integration. Cooperative communication among all members within a heterogeneous setting is necessary for the general successful socioacademic achievement of the classroom members. *Therefore, for successful socioacademic achievement to occur at the classroom level, integration necessarily precedes learning, yet both unequivocally depend upon a resultant commitment by the students and teacher to work and talk together in the form of a cooperative unit as a means to effective learning.*

A Proposed Minimal Criterion for Learning Contexts

Within our model of socioacademic achievement, and to paraphrase Allport (1954), integration never results solely from heterogeneous learners being placed within the same physical context. In like manner, from a Vygotskian social learning perspective, cooperation subsumes individualized learning, thereby having a definite subordinate role in the learning process sequence. From a social learning perspective, an individual student's internalization of knowledge is primordially a function of successfully performing a task with the assistance of a teacher or more capable peer *followed by* individual practice on a similar task until that task can be performed independently. In effect, our model of successful learning in heterogeneous classroom settings extends the basic principles which drive the concepts of integration and communication as initially posited by Allport and Vygotsky, respectively. The functional presence of these principles, then, constitute the minimal criterion for successful instruction and learning involving heterogeneous student populations.

Proposed Ultimate and Minimal Criteria for Teaching in Heterogeneous Contexts

Heterogeneity increasingly typifies the composition of U.S. public school classroom settings. Recent immigrant minority groups characterized by a single common language (e.g., Hispanic), immigrant groups under one ethnic label but representing many language groups and dialects (e.g., Asian), and other designated minority groups (e.g., black, native American, and, again, Hispanic), continue to grow at a collective rate which outpaces that of their white, mainly Anglo American, counterparts. Accordingly, heterogeneity *cannot* serve as a rationale for teachers to not meet the educational needs of all students within their classroom setting. Thus, the ultimate criterion for evaluating successful teaching is that all students achieve to their greatest potential, while the minimum criterion is that the instructional context provide the opportunities for all students to achieve to their greatest potential. A corollary to the above maxims is that existing differences in learning potential among students are essentially insignificant. Successful teaching at the mass level, however, cannot occur in a vacuum, and must rely upon active institutional support and leadership of the type described in chapter 3.

The Roles of Cooperation, Individualization, and Competition

Schooling must be first and foremost cooperative since cooperation promotes and develops the kind of social interaction that celebrates, engenders and develops integration and communication. The role of individualized learning, then, can only be subsumed within the cooperative-learning model which we have presented; however, as a free-standing instructional practice the relevancy of individualized learning is sufficiently weakened as to be discredited. The role of competition in schools must change if integration and communication among ethnically and racially diverse student peers are to lead to successful socioacademic performance at both individual and collective levels. There is scant evidence, at best, to support the value of competition as an instructional element.

Obstacles to Realizing the Socioacademic Achievement Model

In this work, we have attempted to justify and establish a conceptual framework which is educationally appropriate for the present and future heterogeneous composition of our students and society. There are, nevertheless, serious obstacles to implementing this type of alternative educational framework.

First, in the United States our social and legal traditions of education tend toward the segregative rather than integrative, at the classroom level as well as between schools. Furthermore, at the societal level, issues of segregation and racism continue to spark bitter debate, to cause physical and sociopsychological harm to individuals and groups, to cloud group commonalities, and to excite perceived divisions. This conflict serves only to rend the dynamic, yet delicate, threads of our national fabric, rather than enabling it to be tailored to fit our democratic persona.

Second, the notions of competition and individualism are virtually sacred and firmly entrenched in the U.S. ethos, as well as interwoven with, and consequently confounded by, the economic rhetoric of free market enterprise. Lifting oneself up by one's bootstraps is valued, academically and economically, while notions of providing active support to whole groups within the United States, despite the fact of need, are questioned, even rejected, at the philosophic and legal levels.

Third, burgeoning within-group differences at the school site level make social integration, communication and cooperation a more difficult process. Labels such as "Hispanic" quickly lose their definitional power under such circumstances, as students define themselves in other, more culturally divisive ways, even though they seemingly belong to the same ethnic group.

These three elements, alone or in combination, present formidable barriers to effective educational innovation at the classroom or institutional level.

Elements Supporting the Socioacademic Achievement Model

In juxtaposition to the above barriers however, are those elements that can promote and sustain successful socioacademic achievement. Institutional support at the school site and district levels, teacher expertise and commitment, enrichment-based, discovery-oriented curricula which are integrated within and between grades, are three key elements. Each is required to effectively implement and sustain educationally-related integration, communication, and cooperation among students from heterogeneous backgrounds.

Additionally, educational contexts must incorporate the notions and practice of flexible structuring and nonintrusive monitoring of tasks and groupings. The common practice of *laissez-faire* instructional methodologies and activities is not presently compatible with heterogeneous groupings in that it does not support successful socioacademic achievement at the group level. Teachers must still be responsible for the learning context, its structural design and the elements contained within it. Teachers must also be responsible at the programmatic level for what they want the children to learn. The socioacademic achievement model proposes that the elements of integration, communication and cooperation be present and effectively interrelated in each of the above teacher responsibilities. Upon implementation, teachers must maintain an engaging scrutiny with respect to activities and behaviors within groupings in order that they better understand those factors which lead to success and those which require modification or change.

The Role of Computer Technology in Socioacademic Learning

The use of technology poses a threat to group socioacademic success only insofar as educational policy relegates its use toward divisive rather than integrative means or ends. The role of computerized drill-and-practice in the curricula must significantly diminish relative to the enrichment and discovery uses of computer-integrated instructional opportunities. By the same token, educators must require and have access to computers and educational software that will provide enrichment-based, discovery-oriented learning opportunities for their students. The above conditions must hold true wherever computers are used or to be used, regardless of the students' socioeconomic status, race, ethnicity, language of communication, age, or gender, or the relative wealth of their school site. Educational equity, then, is intimately and irreversibly tied to computer-integrated instructional technology. Without equity in the use of technology for instructional purposes, the existing disparities in academic achievement between groups can and will only widen.

Summary

Our purpose has been to offer a framework for establishing educational equity among heterogeneous groups within the same learning context through instructional practices that value the conjoint use of integration, communication, and cooperation as a means to successful academic achievement. Within this framework, educational outcomes are socially interdependent in that success at the individual level is directly related to the social interaction activities experienced during the learning process. For this reason, and to reinforce the value we place on social learning, we have termed any one student's potential learning gains as his or her successful socioacademic achievement.

The ultimate vision which educators must never lose sight of is of course that education in the United States must be a collective enterprise for the collective good. Computers appear to be the most powerful technical instrument available, as a free-standing unit or as the major component of a multi-media system, to support the above vision provided that the instructionally related contents are worthwhile and widespread. Computers, however, will not solve in the foreseeable future how the present problem of human diversity in U.S. schools can be converted to a future national treasure. We feel that this conversion process, if it is to transpire, will decidedly be a result of human enterprise involving the elements of integration, communication and cooperation. It has been the aim of this work to contribute conceptually toward meeting this complex, urgent, and vital educational need, in both its technological and human manifestations, while preserving our democratic heritage.

References

Allen, V. G. (1986). Developing contexts to support second language acquisition. *Language Arts*, 63(1), 61–66

Allport, G. W. (1954). *The nature of prejudice* (1958 ed.). New York: Doubleday Anchor.

Alvarez, L. (1991). Home and school contexts for language development: The experience of two Mexican-origin preschoolers. In M. McGroarty & C. Faltis (Eds.), *In the interest of language: Contexts for learning and using language*. Berlin: Mouton de Gruyer.

Alvarez, L. Pease & Vasquez, O. Artamesia (1990). Sharing language and technical expertise around the computer. In C. J. Faltis & R. A. DeVillar (Eds.), *Language minority students and computers*. Binghamton, NY: Haworth Press.

American Heritage Dictionary (2nd college edition) (1985). Boston: Houghton Mifflin.

Amidon, E. J. & Hough, J. B. (Eds.) (1967). *Interaction analysis: Theory, research and application*. Reading: Addison-Wesley.

Amidon, E. J. & Hough, J. B. (1967). "Chapter overview," in E. J. Amidon and J. B. Hough (Eds.), *Interaction analysis: Theory, research and application*. Reading: Addison-Wesley, 2–3.

Applebee, A., & Langer, J. (1983). Instructional scaffolding: Reading and writing as natural language activities. *Language Arts*, 60(2), 168–175.

Arias, M. B. (1990). Computer access for Hispanic secondary students. In C. J. Faltis and R. A. DeVillar (Eds.), *Language minority students and computers*. Binghamton, NY: Haworth Press.

Arias, M. B. (1986). The context of education for Hispanic students: An overview. In "The education of Hispanic Americans: A challenge for the future," *American Journal of Education*, 97(1), 26–57.

Aronson, E., Blaney, N., Stephan, C., Sikes, J., & Snapp, M. (1978). *The jigsaw classroom*. Beverly Hills: Sage.

Aronson, E. & Osherow, N. (1980). Cooperation, prosocial behavior, and academic performance: experiments in the desegregated classroom. In

R. Slavin, S. Sharan, S. Kagan, R. H. Lazarowitz, C. Webb, and R. Schmuck (Eds.), *Learning to cooperate, cooperating to learn*. New York: Plenum Press, 163–196.

Astik, T. R. (1988). "The courts and education." In F. Schultz (Ed.), *Education 88/89*. The Annual Editions Series. Guildford: Dushkin Publishing, 144–151. From The World & I, March, 1986, 661–675. Reprinted from E. M. Gardner (Ed.). *A new agenda for education*. Washington, D.C.: Heritage Foundation, 1985.

Au, K. H. (1979). Using the experience-text-relationship method with minority children. *Reading Teacher*, 32(6), 677–679.

Au, K. H., & Mason, J. A. (1981). Social organizational factors in learning to read: The balance of rights hypothesis. *Reading Research Quarterly*, 17(1), 115–152.

Au, K. H., & Kawakami, A. J. (1984). Vygotskian perspectives on discussion processes in small-group reading lessons. In P.L. Peterson, L.C. Wilkinson, & M. Hallinan (Eds.). *The social context of instruction: Group organization and group processes*. New York: Academic Press, 209–225.

Au, K. H., Kawakami, A. J. (1985). Research currents: Talk story and learning to read. *Language Arts*, 62(4), 406–411.

Barnes, D. (1976). *From communication to curriculum*. London: Penguin.

Barrera, M. (1979). *Race and class in the Southwest, a theory of racial inequality*. Notre Dame: University of Notre Dame Press.

Becker, H. J. (n.d.). The impact of computer use on children's learning, what research has shown and what it has not. Baltimore: Center for Research on Elementary and Middle Schools, 1–20.

Becker, H. J. (1985). How schools use microcomputers: results from a national survey. In M. Chen & W. Paisley (Eds.), *Children and microcomputers*. Beverly Hills: Sage, 87–107.

Becker, H. J. (1984/1985). School uses of microcomputers: report #6 from a national survey, *Journal of Computers in Mathematics and Science Teaching*, iv(2), 42–49.

Borjas, G. J. & Tienda, M. (1987). The economic consequences of immigration. *Science, 235*, 645–651.

Bork, A. (1979). Interactive learning. Reprinted in R. P. Taylor (Ed.) *The computer in the school: Tutor, tool, tutee*. New York: Teachers College Press, 1980, 53–66.

Bork, A. (1980). Preparing student-computer dialogs: advice to teachers. In R. P. Taylor (Ed.) *The computer in the school: Tutor, tool, tutee.* New York: Teachers College Press, 15–52. (Unpublished version of paper originally circulated by Irvine Physics Computer Development Project, 1978, 1979).

Bork, A. (1985). Children and interactive learning environments. In M. Chen & W. Paisley (Eds.), *Children and microcomputers.* Beverly Hills: Sage, 267–275.

Bouvier, L. F. & Gardner, R. W. (1986). Immigration to the U.S.: The unfinished story. *Population Bulletin,* 41(4). Washington, D.C.: Population Reference Bureau.

Bracy, J. H., Meier, A. & Redwick, E. (Eds.) (1970). *Black nationalism in America.* Indianapolis: Bobbs-Merrill.

Brown v. Board of Education, 347 U.S. 483 (1954).

Brown, A., & Palincsar, A. S. (1986). *Guided, cooperative learning and individual knowledge acquisition.* Technical Report N. 372, Center for the Study of Reading. Urbana: University of Illinois.

Brown, K. & Sayers, D. (n.d.). De Orilla a orilla—From shore to shore: A multilingual, cross-cultural network for cooperative learning. Brochure available from New England Multicultural Resource Center, University of Hartford.

Bruce, B., Michaels, S., & Watson-Gegeo, K. (1985). How computers can change the writing process. *Language Arts, 62*(2), 143–149.

Brumfit, C. (1985). *Communicative methodology in language teaching, the roles of fluency and accuracy.* Cambridge, England: Cambridge University Press, 1984; reprinted, 1985.

Bruner, J. (1978). The role of dialogue in language acquisition. In A. Sinclair, R. Jarvelle, & W. Levelt (Eds.), *The child's concept of language.* New York: Springer-Verlag, 241–256.

Bruner, J. (1981). Interaction and language acquisition. In D. William (Ed.), *The child's construction of language.* New York: Academic Press.

Bruner, J. (1983). *Child's talk.* New York: Norton.

Calfee, R., Avelar La Salle, R., & Cancino, H. (1988). Accelerating language and literacy for educationally at-risk students. Paper presented at Accelerating the Education of At-Risk Students conference, Stanford University, November 17–18, 1988.

Calfee, R., Cazden, C., Duran, R., Griffin, M., Martus, M., & Willis, H. (1981). *Designing reading instruction for cultural minorities: The case of the Kamehameha early education program.* Report to the Ford Foundation, December. ED 215 039.

Catterall, J. & Cota-Robles, E. (1988). Demography of at-risk students and the social consequences. Paper presented at Accelerating the Education of At-Risk Students Conference, Stanford University, November 17–18, 1988.

Cazden, C. (1981). Performance before competence: Assistance to child discourse in the zone of proximal development. *Newsletter of the Laboratory of Comparative Human Cognition*, 3 (1), 5–8.

Cazden, C. (1988). *Classroom discourse: The language of teaching and learning.* Portsmouth: Heinemann.

Cohen, E. G. (1975). The effects of desegregation on race relations. *Law and Contemporary Problems*, 39, 271–299.

Cohen, E. G. & Arias, M. B. (1988). Accelerating the education of language minority at-risk students. Paper presented at Accelerating the Education of At-Risk Students Conference, Stanford University, November 17–18, 1988.

Commission on Work, Family and Citizenship (1988). *The forgotten half: Pathways to success for America's youth and young families.* Washington, D.C.: William T. Grant Foundation.

Connor, W. (1985). *Mexican-Americans in comparative perspective.* Washington, D.C.: Urban Institute Press.

Connor, W. (1985). Who are the Mexican-Americans? A note on comparability. In Connor, W. (Ed.), *Mexican-Americans in comparative perspective.* Washington, D.C.: Urban Institute Press.

Cook, S. W. (1984). The 1954 social science statement and school desegregation: A reply to Gerard. *American Psychologist*, 39, 819–832.

Cook, S. W. (1969). Motives in a conceptual analysis of attitude-related behavior. In W. Arnold and D. Levine (Eds.), *Nebraska Symposium on Motivation*, 17. Lincoln: University of Nebraska Press, 179–236.

Crain, R., Mahard, R. E., & Narot, R. E. (1982). *Making desegregation work: how schools create social climates.* Cambridge: Ballinger.

Cuban, L. (1986). *Teachers and machines.* New York: Teachers College Press.

Cuban, L. (1984). *How teachers taught: Constancy and change in American classrooms 1890–1980*. New York: Longmans.

Cummins, J. & Sayers, D. (1990). Education 2001: Learning networks and educational reform. In C. J. Faltis & R. A. DeVillar (Eds.), *Language minority students and computers*. Binghamton, NY: Haworth Press.

Cushman, R. F. (1975). *Cases in constitutional law (4th edition)*. Englewood Cliffs: Prentice-Hall.

Davis, C., Haub, C. & Willette, J. (1983). U.S. Hispanics: Changing the face of America. *Population Bulletin*, 38(3), June, 1983.

Dawe, H. C. (1934). Raising standards of behavior in the kindergarten. *Elementary School Journal, 35*, 267–280.

DeAvila, E. A., Duncan, S. E., & Navarrete, C. J. (1987). Cooperative learning: Integrating language and content-area instruction. In L. Valdez Pierce (Ed.), *Teacher resource guide series*. Wheaton: The National Clearinghouse for Bilingual Education.

Deutscher, M. & Chein, I. (1948). The psychological effects of enforced segregation: A survey of social science opinion. *Journal of Psychology*, 26, 259–287.

DeVillar, R. A. (1990). Second language use within the nontraditional classroom: Computers, cooperative learning, and bilingualism. In R. Jacobson & C. Faltis (Eds.), *Language distribution issues in bilingual schooling*. Clevedon, England: Multilingual Matters, Ltd., 133–159.

DeVillar, R. A. (1989). Computers, software, and cooperative learning: Working together to the benefit of the language minority student. In J. H. Collins, N. Estes, W. D. Gattis, & D. Walker (Eds.), *Proceedings of the Sixth International Conference on Technology and Education* (2 vols). Edinburgh, Scotland: CEP Consultants, Ltd., 367–370.

DeVillar, R. A. (1988). Integrating instructional objectives, strategies & technologies: Opportunities for concurrent second language development and subject matter mastery in a CAI, cooperative learning setting. In J. H. Collins, N. Estes, & D. Walker (Eds.), *Proceedings of the Fifth International Conference on Technology and Education* (2 vols). Edinburgh, Scotland: CEP Consultants, Ltd., 514–517.

DeVillar, R. A. (1987). Variation in the language use of peer dyads within a bilingual, cooperative, computer-assisted instructional setting. Unpublished doctoral dissertation, Stanford University.

DeVillar, R. A. (1986). Computers and educational equity in U.S. schools.

Paper prepared for Stanford University-Unesco International Symposium on Computers and Education, March 12–16, 1986, Stanford, CA.

DeVillar, R. A. and Faltis, C. J. (1987). Computers and educational equity in American public schools. In *Capstone Journal of Education viii*(4), 1–8.

DeVries, D. L. & Slavin, R. E. (1978). Teams-Games-Tournament (TGT): Review of ten classroom experiments. In *Journal of Research and Development in Education*, 12, 28–38.

Dewey, J. (1916). *Democracy and education*. New York: Macmillan.

Drake, St. Clair (1965). The social and economic status of the Negro in the United States. In *DÆDALUS, Journal of the American Academy of Arts and Sciences 94*(4), 771–814.

DuBois, R. D. (1950). *Neighbors in action*. New York: Harper.

Dwyer, T. (1974a). Heuristic strategies for using computers to enrich education. Reprinted in R. P. Taylor (Ed.), *The computer in the school: Tutor, tool, tutee*. New York: Teachers College Press, 1980, 87–103.

Dwyer, T. (1974b). The significance of solo-mode computing for curriculum design. Reprinted in R. P. Taylor (Ed.). *The computer in the school: Tutor, tool, tutee*. New York: Teachers College Press, 1980, 104–112.

Dwyer, T. (1975). Some thoughts on computers and greatness in teaching. Reprinted in R. P. Taylor (Ed.) *The computer in the school: Tutor, tool, tutee*. New York: Teachers College Press, 1980, 113–118.

Dwyer, T. (1976). The fundamental problem of computer-enhanced education and some ideas about a solution. Reprinted in R. P. Taylor (Ed.), *The computer in the school: Tutor, tool, tutee*. New York: Teachers College Press, 1980, 119–125.

Edfelt, N. (1989). Computer assisted second language acquisition: The oral discourse of children at the computer in a cooperative learning context. Unpublished doctoral dissertation, Stanford University.

Edfelt, N. (1990). Oral interaction and collaboration at the computer: learning English as a second language with the help of your peers. In C. F. Faltis & R. A. DeVillar (Eds.), *Language minority students and computers*. Binghamton, NY: Haworth Press

Enright, D. S., & McCloskey, M. L. (1988). *Integrating English: Developing English language and literacy in the multilingual classroom*. Reading: Addison-Wesley.

Epstein, J. L. (1985). After the bus arrives: Resegregation in desegregated schools. *Journal of Social Issues 41*(3), 23–43.

Faltis, C. (1984). Sway students in the foreign language classroom. *Foreign Language Annals, 19*(2), 195–202.

Faltis, C. J. & DeVillar, R. A. (Eds.) (in press). *Language minority students and computers.* Binghamton, NY: Haworth Press.

Faltis, C. J. & DeVillar, R. A. (1990). Computer uses for teaching Spanish to bilingual native speakers. In C. J. Faltis & R. A. DeVillar (Eds.), *Language minority students and computers.* Binghamton, NY: Haworth Press.

Flanders, N. (1970). *Analyzing teaching behavior.* London: Addison-Wesley.

Forman, E. & Cazden, C. (1985). Exploring Vygotskian perspectives in education: The cognitive value of peer interaction. In J. Wertsch (Ed.), *Culture, communication, and cognition: Vygotskian perspectives.* Cambridge, England: Cambridge University Press.

Fordham, S. (1988). Racelessness as a factor in Black students' success: Pragmatic strategy or Pyrrhic victory? *Harvard Educational Review, 58*(1), 54–84.

Franklin, J. H. (1965). The two worlds of race: A historical view. In *DÆDALUS, Journal of the American Academy of Arts and Sciences, 94*(4), 899–948.

Franz, G. & Papert, S. (1988). Computer as material: Messing about with time. *Teachers College Record, 89*(3), 408–417.

Furst, N. & Amidon, E. (1962). Teacher-pupil interaction patterns in the elementary school. Reprinted in E. Amidon & E. J. Hough (Eds.), *Interaction analysis: Theory, research and application.* Reading: Addison-Wesley, 1967, 167–175.

Gaies, S. (1985). *Peer involvement in language learning.* Orlando: Harcourt Brace Jovanovich.

Gann, L. H. & Duignan, P. H. (1986). *The Hispanics in the United States, A history.* Boulder: Westview Press and Stanford, California: Hoover Institution on War, Revolution and Peace.

Garcia, E. (1990). Instructional discourse in "effective" Hispanic classrooms. In R. Jacobson, & C. Faltis (Eds.), *Language distribution issues in bilingual schooling.* Clevedon, England: Multilingual Matters, 104–120.

General Accounting Office (1987). *Bilingual education: Information on limited English proficient students*. Washington, D.C.: Author.

Goffman, E. (1981). *Forms of talk*. Philadelphia: University of Pennsylvania Press, 2nd printing, 1983.

Goodlad, J. (1984). *A place called school: Prospects for the future*. New York: McGraw-Hill.

Greeno, J. G. (1989). A perspective on thinking. *American Psychologist, 44*(2), 134–142.

Grice, H. P. (1975). Logic and conversation. In P. Cole & J. L. Morgan (Eds.), *Syntax and semantics, speech acts* (vol. 3). New York: Academic Press, 41–58.

Hallinan, M. T. & Teixeira, R. A. (1987). Students' interracial friendships: Individual characteristics, structural effects, and racial differences. In *American Journal of Education, 95*(4), 563–583.

Hawkins, B. (1988). Scaffolded classroom interaction in a language minority setting. Unpublished doctoral dissertation, University of California, Los Angeles.

Hawkins, J. and Sheingold, K. (1986). Computers and the organization of learning in Classrooms. In J. A. Culbertson and L. L. Cunningham (Eds.), *Microcomputers in education, part 1*. Chicago: University of Chicago Press, 40–58.

Heath, S. B. (1989). The learner as cultural member. In M. Rice & R. Schiefelbusch (Eds.), *The teachability of language*. Baltimore: Paul H. Brookes, 333–350.

Hernandez-Chavez, E. (1972). Early code-separation in the second language speech of Spanish-speaking children. Paper presented at the Stanford Child Language Research Forum, Stanford University, Stanford, California.

Johnson, D. W. and Johnson, R. T. (1981). Effects of cooperative and individualistic learning experiences on interethnic interaction. In *Journal of Educational Psychology, 73*(3), 444–449.

Johnson, D. W., Johnson, R. T., & Holubec, E. Johnson (1986). *Revised circles of learning: Cooperation in the classroom*. Edina, Minnesota: Interaction Book Company.

Johnson, D. W., Johnson, R. T., Holubec, E. Johnson, & Roy, P. (1984). *Circles of learning, Cooperation in the classroom*. Alexandria: Association for Supervision and Curriculum Development.

Johnson, D. W., Johnson, R. T., Holubec, E. Johnson, & Roy, P. (1988). *Circles of learning, Cooperation in the classroom*. Alexandria: Association for Supervision and Curriculum Development (Original work published 1984).

Johnson, R. T., Johnson, D. W., & Stanne, M. B. (1986). Comparison of computer-assisted cooperative, competitive, and individualistic learning. *American Educational Research Journal, 23*(3), 382–392.

Johnson, G. M. (1969). *Education law*. East Lansing: Michigan State University.

Kagan, S. (1986). Cooperative learning and sociocultural factors in schooling. In *Beyond language: Social and cultural factors in schooling language minority students*. Los Angeles: Evaluation, Dissemination and Assessment Center, California State University, Los Angeles.

Kinder, D. R. (1986). The continuing American dilemma: White resistance to racial change 40 years after Myrdal. In *Journal of Social Issues, 42*(2), 151–171.

Klineberg, O. (1986). SPSSI and race relations, in the 1950s and after. In *Journal of Social Issues, 42*(4), 53–59.

Krashen, S. (1982). *Principles and practices in second language acquisition*: Oxford: Pergamon Press.

Krashen, S. (1985). *The input hypothesis: Issues and implications*. London: Longman Press.

Laboratory of Comparative Human Cognition (1989). Kids and computers: A positive vision of the future. *Harvard Educational Review, 59*(1), 73–86.

Langer, J. (1987). A sociocognitive perspective on literacy. In J. Langer (Ed.), *Language, literacy and culture: Issues in society and schooling*. Norwood: Ablex, 1–20.

Levin, H. J. (1985). *The educationally disadvantaged: A national crisis* (Prog. Rep. No. 85–B1). Stanford: School of Education, Stanford University, Institute for Research on Education Finance and Governance.

Levin, H., Glass, G. V., & Meister, G. R. (1984). *Cost effectiveness of four educational interventions* (Proj. Rep. No. 84–A11). Stanford: School of Education, Stanford University, Institute for Research on Educational Finance and Governance.

Lockard, D. & Murphy, W. (1980). *Basic cases in constitutional law*. New York: Macmillan.

Locke, A. (1925). The new Negro. In Locke, A. (Ed.), *The new Negro*. New York: Albert and Charles Boni, 3–16. Reproduced in J. H. Bracey, A. Meier, & E. Rudwick (Eds.), *Black nationalism*. Indianapolis: Bobbs-Merrill, 1970, 334–347.

Long, M. (1981). Input, interaction, and second language acquisition. In H. Winitz (Ed.), *Native language and foreign language acquisition*. Annals of the New York Academy of Sciences No. 379.

Long, M., & Porter, P. (1985). Group work, interlanguage talk, and second language acquisition. *TESOL Quarterly, 19*(2), 207–228.

Maddux, C. D. (1989). Logo: Scientific dedication or religious fanaticism in the 1990s? *Educational Technology*, February, 18–23.

Maddux, C. D. & Cummings, R. W. (1987). Equity for the mildly handicapped. *The Computing Teacher, 14*(5), 16–17, 49.

Male, M., Johnson, R., Johnson, D., & Anderson, M. (1986). *Cooperative learning and computers: An activity guide for teachers*. Santa Cruz: Educational Apple-cations.

Mason, J. M., & Au, K. H. (1986). *Reading instruction for today*. Glenview: Scott, Foresman and Company.

Matute-Bianchi, M. E. (1986). Ethnic identities and patterns of school success and failure among Mexican-descent and Japanese-American students in a California high school: An ethnographic analysis. In M. B. Arias (Ed.), The education of Hispanic Americans: A challenge for the future, *American Journal of Education, 97*(1), 233–255.

McCarthy, C. (1988). Rethinking liberal and radical perspectives on racial inequality in schooling: Making the case for nonsynchrony. In *Harvard Educational Review, 58*(3), 265–279.

McGroarty, M. (1989). The benefits of cooperative learning arrangements in second language instruction. *NABE Journal, 13*(2), 127–144.

Mehan, H. (1979). *Learning Lessons*. Cambridge: Harvard University Press.

Merino, B., Legarreta, D., Coughran, C., & Hoskins, J. (1990). Interaction at the computer by language minority boys and girls paired with fluent English proficient peers. In C. J. Faltis & R. A. DeVillar (Eds.), *Language minority students and computers*. Binghamton, NY: Haworth Press

Miller, N., Brewer, M. B. & Edwards, K. (1985). Cooperative interaction in desegregated settings: A laboratory analogue. *Journal of Social Issues, 41*(3), 63–79.

Milk, R. (1980). Variations in language use patterns across different group settings in two bilingual second grade classrooms. Unpublished doctoral dissertation, Stanford University.

Moll, L. C. (1988). Some key issues in teaching Latino students. *Language Arts, 65*(5), 465–472.

Monti, D. J. (1986). *Brown's* velvet cushion: Metropolitan desegregation and the politics of illusion. *Metropolitan Education*, 1, Spring, 52–64.

Moore, J. and Pachon, H. (1985). *Hispanics in the United States.* Englewood Cliffs: Prentice-Hall.

Morris, A. A. (1974). *The Constitution and American education.* St. Paul: West Publishing Series.

National Assessment of Educational Progress (1985). The reading report card: *Progress toward excellence in our schools: Trends in reading over four national assessments*, 1971–1984. Princeton: Educational Testing Service.

National Coalition of Advocates for Students 91985). *Barriers of excellence: Our children at risk.* Boston: Author.

National Science Foundation (1978). *Report of the 1977 national survey of science, mathematics, and social studies education.* Washington, D.C.: National Science Foundation.

Navarro, R. A. (1986). A silent scream: An essay review of *"Make something happen:" Hispanics and urban high school reform* (2 vols.). In *Metropolitan Education*, 1, Spring, 119–126.

Neves, H. A. (1984). Talking in the classroom and second language acquisition. Unpublished doctoral dissertation, Stanford University.

Nix, D. (1988). Should computers know what you can do with them? *Teachers College Record, 89*(3), 418–430.

O'Hare, W. P. (1988). *The rise of poverty in rural America.* Occasional paper, Population Trends and Public Policy. Washington, D.C.: Population Reference Bureau, Inc. (July).

Orfield, G. (1986). Knowledge, ideology, and school desegregation: Views through different prisms. In *Metropolitan Education*, 1, Spring, 92–99.

Oxford-Carpenter, R., Pol, L., Lopez, D. Stupp, P., Gendell, M., & Peng, S. (1984). *Demographic projections of non-English-language-background and limited-English-proficient persons in the United States to the year 2000 by state, age, and language group.* Rosslyn: InterAmerica Research Associates.

Palincsar, A. S. (1986). The role of dialogue in providing scaffolded instruction. *Educational Psychologist*, 21(1 & 2), 73–98.

Palincsar, A. S. & Brown, A. (1984). Reciprocal teaching of comprehension-fostering and comprehension-monitoring activities. *Cognition and Instruction*, 1(2), 117–175.

Palincsar, A. S., Brown, A., & Campione, J. (1989). Discourse as a mechanism for acquiring process and knowledge. Paper presented at the American Association of Research in Education, San Francisco, March 28.

Pankratz, R. (1967). Verbal interaction patterns in the classrooms of selected physics teachers. In E. J. Amidon and J. B. Hough (Eds.), *Interaction analysis: Theory, research, and application*. Reading: Addison-Wesley, 189–209.

Papert, S. (1980). *Mindstorms*. New York: Basic Books.

Papert, S. (1970). Teaching children thinking. Reprinted in R. P. Taylor (Ed.), *The computer in the school: Tutor, tool, tutee*. New York: Teachers College Press, 1980, 161–176.

Papert, S. (1978). Personal computing and its impact on education. Reprinted in R. P. Taylor (Ed.). *The computer in the school: Tutor, tool, tutee*. New York: Teachers College Press, 1980, 197–202.

Papert, S. (1980). Computer-based microworlds as incubators for powerful ideas. In R. P. Taylor (Ed.), *The computer in the school: Tutor, tool, tutee*. New York: Teachers College Press, 203–210.

Pienemann, M. (1984). Psychological constraints on the teachability of languages. *Studies in Second Language Acquisition*, 6, 186–214.

Perret-Clermont, A. (1980). *Social interaction and cognitive development in children*. New York: Academic Press.

Plank, D. N. & Turner, M. (1987). Changing patterns in black school politics: Atlanta, 1872–1973. In *American Journal of Education*, 95(4), 584–608.

Ramirez, J. D., & Merino, B. J. (1990). Classroom talk in English immersion, early-exit transitional bilingual education programs. In R. Jacobson & C. Faltis (Eds.), *Language distribution issues in bilingual schooling*. Clevedon, England: Multilingual Matters, 61–103.

Redkey, E. S. (1969). *Black exodus*. New Haven: Yale University Press.

Resnick, L. (1985). Cognition and instruction: Recent theories of human competence and how it is acquired. In B. L. Hammond (Ed.), *Psychology and learning: The Masser lecture series.* Washington, D.C.: American Psychological Association.

Reynolds, W. B. (1986). Education alternatives to transportation failures: The desegregation response to a resegregation dilemma. In *Metropolitan Education*, 1, Spring, 3–14.

Riel, M. (1985). The computer chronicles newswire: A functional learning environment for acquiring literacy skills. *Journal of Educational Computing Research, 1*(3), 317–337.

Rothbart, M. and John, O. P. (1985). Social categorization and behavioral episodes: A cognitive analysis of the effects of intergroup contact. In *Journal of Social Issues, 41*(3), 81–104.

Salinas, G. (1973). Mexican Americans and the desegregation of schools in the southwest. In O. I. Romano-V (Ed.), *Voices, Readings from El Grito* (second edition). Berkeley: Quinto Sol, 366–399.

Salomone, R. C. (1986). *Equal education under law*. New York: St. Martin's Press.

Saracho, O. N. (1982). The effects of a computer-assisted instruction program on basic skills, achievement and attitudes toward instruction of Spanish-speaking migrant children. *American Educational Research Journal*, 19(2), 201–219.

Sayers, D. (1989). Bilingual sister classes in computer writing networks. In D. M. Johnson & D. H. Roen (Eds.). *Richness in Writing: Empowering ESL students*. New York: Longman, 120–133.

Sayers, D. (1988). Interscholastic correspondence exchanges in Celestin Freinet's modern school movement: Implications for computer-mediated student writing networks. Qualifying Paper. Cambridge: Gutman Library, Harvard Graduate School of Education.

Schinke-Llano, L. (1983). Foreigner talk in content classrooms. In H. Seliger & M. Long (Eds.), *Classroom oriented research in language acquisition*. Rowley: Newbury House.

Schwartz, J. L. (1989). Intellectual mirrors: A step in the direction of making schools knowledge-making places. *Harvard Educational Review, 59*(1), 51–61.

Science, Education, and Transportation Program (1987). Trends and status of computers in schools: Use in Chapter 1 programs and use with limited English proficient students. Staff paper. Washington, D.C.: Office of Technology Assessment, U.S. Congress.

Sharan, S., & Sharan, Y. (1976). *Small group teaching*. Englewood Cliffs: Educational Technology Publications.

Sharan, S., & Shachar, H. (1988). *Language and learning in the cooperative classroom*. New York: Springer-Verlag.

Sirotnik, K. A. (1981). What you see is what you get: a summary of observations in over 1000 elementary and secondary classrooms. In Technical Report No. 29. Los Angeles: Graduate School of Education, University of California, Los Angeles.

Skinner, B. F. (1948). *Walden Two* (9th printing). New York: Macmillan, 1961.

Slavin, Robert, E. (1980). Cooperative learning. *In Review of Educational Research, 50,* 315–342.

Slavin, Robert E. (1985). Cooperative learning: Applying contact theory in desegregated schools. In *Journal of Social Issues,* 41(3), 45–62.

Slavin, R. E., Leavey, M., & Madden, N. A. (1984). Combining cooperative learning and individualized instruction: Effects on student mathematics achievement, attitudes, and behaviors. In *Elementary School Journal, 84,* 409–422.

Slavin, R. E. & Oickle, E. (1981). Effects of cooperative learning teams on student achievement and race relations: Treatment by race interactions. *Sociology of Education, 54,* 174–180.

Sniderman, P. M. & Tetlock, P. E. (1986). Symbolic racism: Problems of motive attribution in political analysis. In *Journal of Social Issues,* 42(2), 129–150.

Snyder, T. P. & Palmer, J. (1986). *In search of the most amazing things: Children, education, and computers*. Reading: Addison-Wesley.

Solomon, C. (1986). *Computer environments for children*. Cambridge: MIT Press.

Stephan, W. G. & Brigham, J. C., Eds. (1985). Intergroup contact, *Journal of Social Issues, 41*(3).

Stephan, W. G. & Brigham, J. C. (1985). Introduction. In W. G. Stephan & J. C. Brigham (Eds.), Intergroup Contact. *Journal of Social Issues, 41*(3), 1–8.

Stouffer, S. A. Suchman, E. A., DeVinney, L. C., Star, S. A., & Williams, R. M. (1949). *The American soldier: Adjustment during army life*. Princeton: Princeton University Press.

Suppes, P. (1965). Computer-based mathematics instruction. Reprinted in

R. P. Taylor (Ed.), *The computer in the school: Tutor, tool, tutee.* New York: Teachers College Press, 1980, 215–230.

Suppes, P. (1967). The teacher and computer-assisted instruction. Reprinted in R. P. Taylor (Ed.), *The computer in the school: Tutor, tool, tutee.* New York: Teachers College Press, 1980, 231–235.

Suppes, P. (1975). Impact of computers on curriculum in the schools and universities. Reprinted in R. P. Taylor (Ed.), *The computer in the school: Tutor, tool, tutee.* New York: Teachers College Press, 1980, 236–247.

Suppes, P. (1978). The future of computers in education. Reprinted in R. P. Taylor (Ed.), *The computer in the school: Tutor, tool, tutee. New York*: Teachers College Press, 1980, 248–261.

Swain, M. (1985). Communicative competence: Some roles of comprehensible input and comprehensible output in its development. In S. Gass & C. Madden (Eds.), *Input in second language acquisition.* Rowley: Newbury House, 1985.

Tatel, D. S., Lanigan, J. & Sneed, M. F. (1986). The fourth decade of *Brown*: Metropolitan desegregation and quality of education. In *Metropolitan Education*, 1, Spring, 15–35.

Taylor, R. P., Ed. (1980), *The computer in the school.* New York: Teachers College Press.

Tharp, R. & Gallimore, R. (1988). *Rousing minds to life.* Cambridge, England: Cambridge University Press.

Trueba, H. T. (1989) *Raising silent voices: Educating the linguistic minorities for the 21st century.* New York: Newbury House.

Vygotsky, L. S. (1934). *Thinking and speech: Psychological investigations.* Moscow and Leningrad: Gosudarstvennoe Sotsail'no-Ekonomicheskoe Izdatel'stvo.

Vygotsky, L. S. (1978). *Mind in society: The development of higher psychological processes.* Cambridge: Harvard University Press.

Waldron, M. (1970, August 30). *The New York Times*, p. 68.

Weigel, R. H., Wiser, P. L., & Cook, S. W. (1975). Impact of cooperative learning experiences on cross-ethnic relations and attitudes. *Journal of Social Issues, 31*(1), 219–245.

Weir, S. (1989). The computer in schools: Machine as humanizer. *Harvard Educational Review, 59*(1), 61–73.

Weisner, T. S., Gallimore, R. & Jordan, C. (1988). Unpackaging cultural effects on classroom learning: Native Hawaiian peer assistance and child-generated activity. *Anthropology and Education Quarterly, 19*(4), 327–353.

Wells, G. (1985). Language and learning: An interactional perspective. In G. Wells & J. Nicholls (Eds.), *Language & learning: An interactional perspective*. London: Falmer.

Wertsch, J. (1985). *Vygotsky and the social formation of mind*. Cambridge: Harvard University Press.

William T. Grant Commission on Work, Family and Citizenship (1988). The forgotten half: Pathways to success for America's youth and young families. In *Phi Delta Kappan, 70*(4), 280–289.

Wollenberg, C. M. (1978). *All deliberate speed, segregation and exclusion in California schools, 1855–1975*. Berkeley: University of California.

Wong-Fillmore, L. (1985). When does teacher talk work as input? In S. M. Gass & C. Madden (Eds.). *Input in second language acquisition*. Rowley: Newbury House, 17–50.

Yinger, J. M. (1985). Assimilation in the United States: The Mexican-Americans. In Connor, Walker (Ed.), *Mexican-Americans in comparative perspective*. Washington, D.C.: Urban Institute Press, 30–55.

Zirkel, P. A. & Richardson, S. N. (1988). *A digest of supreme court decisions affecting education* (2nd edition). Bloomington: Phi Delta Kappa Educational Foundation.

Author Index

Subject Index

Artificial intelligence (AI), 91

Bork, Alfred: model of computer learning, 71-74; fallacies of the model, 72-73; on individual learning, 71-72; on integrating teachers with computer software, 73; and John Henry, 73 Bilingual/English as a second language (ESL) classrooms: characteristics of, 9; compared to regular classrooms, 9; time and quality of talk in, 30

Bilingual programs, types: early-exit transitional, 28n; late-exit transitional, 28n

Calibration, 13, 16; defined, 14; intra-group, 25. See also Second language acquisiton.

Chicano, 45, 46. See also Hispanics in U.S.

Cholo, 45, 46. See also Hispanics in U.S.

Classroom grouping strategies. See Whole class instruction; Small group instruction; individualized instruction

Classroom language: characteristics of, 29. See also whole class instruction; Bilingual/ESL classrooms

Commission on Work, Family, and Citizenship, 35

Common Ground, 121

Communicative events, key assumptions of, 6, 7

Comprehensible input: defined 23; compared to the zone of proximal development, 23, 24. See Zone of proximal development

Computer as material model, 87. See Franz and Papart

Computer as production studio model, 90. See Nix

Computer Chronicle Network (CCN), 113-155

Computer-Integrated Instruction: alternative to remedial instruction, 110; and Chapter 1 students, 106; early practices, 71-86; Enrichment-based for limited English proficient students, 113; and limited English proficient students, 105, 106; minimal necessary condition for socio-academic success, 28; pedagogical limitations of remediation, 109; remedial programs, 105; role of language in, 111

Computers: as an educational alternative, xi, xii

Computers: as tools for cooperative learning, viii

Cooperative learning: as an educational alternative, 30; and contact theory, 53, 59; essential elements of, 66; and friendship patterns, 55, 56; historical antecedents, 30-35

Cooperative learning methods, 53, Student teams-achievement divisions (STAD), 53; Team-Assisted Individualization (TAI), 54; Teams-Games-Tournaments